CLARKSON POTTER/PUBLISHERS
NEW YORK

TREJO'S TACOS

RECIPES AND STORIES FROM L.A.

by DANNY TREJO
with HUGH GARVEY

photographs by ED ANDERSON

This book is dedicated to my family.

First and foremost, to the memory of my mother. We finally got our restaurant, Mom.

Second, to my kids. It's for you I do everything. I love you.

CONTENTS

ONCE UPON A TIME *in* LOS ANGELES

How does a man known for playing merciless, shirtless, tattooed, gun-toting, vengeance-thirsty, knife-throwing tough guys become the face of a restaurant group selling award-winning tacos, authentic *barbacoa*, and kale salad? I say this a lot and Trejo's Tacos is proof of it: It's not how you start. It's how you finish.

While I play "the bad guy" in movies, I've been a lot of things over the years, including a boxer, a bodybuilder, a drug counselor, and, for a while, a real bad guy—which is how I ended up in San Quentin and Soledad state prisons in the 1960s. It was in prison that I got clean and sober. That was just one chapter in my story—since then, I have been in over three hundred movies, became a father to three kids, and acquired a collection of lowriders, vintage cars, and motorcycles. I still go to the penitentiaries, but now I'm on the other side of the bars as a drug counselor. I've traveled around the world at least ten times for my job, but I always come back home to Los Angeles. My life today is very different from what it was in the 1960s. I used to rob restaurants. Today I own eight of them. And we keep growing, with restaurants from Pasadena to Hollywood and LAX to Woodland Hills.

But back to where I started. Home for me in the 1950s and '60s was a mixed bag to say the least. I grew up in Echo Park long before it became a hipster neighborhood. My family moved to Pacoima in the northeastern corner of the San Fernando Valley, where the sprawl of the L.A. grid glitters until it goes dark against the Angeles National Forest. When I wasn't in prison or getting into trouble, there was always home, and I was always welcome. Even more important than home was Mom, who, no matter whether I was being good or bad, would cook the best food. I loved it. Trejo's Tacos exists because of that love.

My mom was a killer cook. Back in the 1950s in working-class Latino families—heck, in most working families—it went like this: At the first of the month we would have these elaborate, unbelievable meals: chicken mole, carne asada, and enchiladas stacked high like they do in Texas, where my mom was from. But then by the end of the month, when the money was running out and the rent was due, the dishes wouldn't have proper names. Mom

started making food with whatever we had left in the cupboard. We'd ask, "Ma, what is this?" She'd say, "It doesn't matter. I just mixed it, you know." The next night we'd ask and she'd say, "It's out of the cupboard." The next night she'd say, "Just eat it. It's good for you." And it always was.

These meals are some of my best memories of growing up. We would also have chorizo and eggs for breakfast. Nopales. Chicharrón she'd cook in a green chile sauce and then mix with eggs. Migas stewed until the tortillas were soft.

My dad didn't share our enthusiasm for food. He'd come home from work and he would just eat. My dad was the Mexican Archie Bunker. He had five brothers. If they made baseball cards for these guys, they would all read "Position: Macho." Back then the thinking was that your wife should stay home and cook. Only in families where the guys couldn't make it on their own did the wives have to work. So when I would say, "Mom, let's open a restaurant!" and we'd talk about what our restaurant would serve and how it would look, my dad would bark: "Why do you need a restaurant? You've got a fully functioning kitchen with a freaking O'Keefe and Merritt stove right there!" (O'Keefe and Merritt stoves were big in the 1950s and now they're collector's items—if you don't believe me, just check eBay.) "Both of you can go in there and cook whatever you want." And so there went that dream.

When I was twelve, my life took a detour when I started hanging out with Uncle Gilbert, my dad's youngest brother. He was my hero—he taught me how to box, and it turned out I was a natural. He was also the guy who got me into drugs and robbing people. We were literal partners in crime. It got to the point where you weren't quite sure if you robbed people to support your drug habit or did drugs to support your robbery habit. Through it all, my mom was always there for me, in the kitchen cooking up carne asada or chilaquiles, no matter what. When I

was out partying with my friends, we'd all show up in my mom's kitchen, sometimes at one, two o'clock in the morning. First, my mom would bawl me out for being out so late. Then she'd make us something to eat with a big smile on her face, thanking God I was home. That kitchen was always a safe haven, a place where I could stay out of trouble.

But I never stayed out of trouble for very long. I ended up doing time for armed robbery and drug dealing. In Soledad and San Quentin I put my boxing skills to good use and became a lightweight and welterweight boxing champion, so I would always eat well. Sometimes I wouldn't even need to go to chow—people would just bring me food. On Saturdays we'd have what we called "spreads," which are kind of like prison picnics, as much as they could be in a place like the pen—a sort of celebration of life, mostly for the guys that didn't get visits because they had a falling out with their family, or their wife or girlfriend left them. We took care of each other—we'd all get together and everybody would bring something. Sort of like a potluck. You know that scene in *Goodfellas* with all the guys sitting around cooking and eating this big Italian feast? It wasn't quite like that. Some guys would bring noodles, some guys would bring loose bread, or chocolate, another guy would bring some smuggled-in hooch or homemade pruno, the booze you make by fermenting sugar and cafeteria scraps. We'd all sit out in the yard and have a picnic.

I was in and out of prison for eleven years, and toward the end of that time, I got sober. I remember it clearly. It was Cinco de Mayo, 1968. I made a vow to get clean and to dedicate myself to helping others. When I got out a year later, I started working with ex-cons and other guys who were trying to get and stay clean, too. I worked construction and became a drug counselor. One day one of the guys I was helping stay clean asked me to go visit him on the set of a movie he was working on. This was the mid-'80s and there were a lot of drugs on set and the guy wanted me to be there and help keep him from using. So I go down to the set and I'm watching them film the movie—it was called *Runaway Train* and Eric Roberts was the star. The movie took place in a prison, so I felt right at home. In a weird twist of fate, the screenwriter happened to be my old pal Eddie Bunker, who did time with me in San Quentin. He recognized me (I kind of stand out) and remembered that I was a boxer. Eddie hired me to train the movie's star, Eric Roberts, how to box. The director of the movie, Andrei Konchalovsky, liked the way I looked and cast me as a fighter. That launched my career. From there I started getting roles—you know, for the characters you see listed in the credits as "bad guy #1," or "scary guy #2," "tough guy #3," you get the gist. I eventually worked my way up to Razor Charlie in Robert Rodriguez and Quentin Tarantino's *From Dusk till Dawn*, Trejo in Michael Mann's *Heat*, and Machete in everything from *Spy Kids* to *Machete Kills*.

So some thirty years and three hundred movies later I'm working on a movie called *Bad Ass* with a producer named Ash Shah. He provided much better craft services—or "crafty," as the movie industry calls on-set catering—than most producers. There were always fresh salads, vegetables, and grilled fish. I like to eat clean and Ash saw that I appreciated the healthy spread. One day we're eating dinner and he asks me outright, "Danny, why don't you open a restaurant?" At that moment I almost heard my mom speaking. I felt chills course through my body. But I didn't really take it seriously, so I just joked, "Sure, and I'd call it Trejo's Tacos!" I was kidding, but Ash wasn't. Six months later Ash came to me with a business plan. And it was a great plan. Over the years we've learned a lot of things about cooking a new kind of L.A.–Mexican food and we want to share it with you.

When we talked about what the restaurant could be, we knew we wanted to make everyone feel welcomed and able to find something delicious to eat. If there's one thing I learned in Hollywood, it's that everyone has some sort of dietary restriction. After you wrap a movie, ten people will all go out to celebrate and they'll have ten different special dietary requests: one person will be gluten-free, the others vegetarian, paleo, keto, vegan, low-carb, and so forth. So when we put the menu together, we made sure that if you've got ten people on ten different diets, everybody's going to still be able to find something satisfying and tasty to eat.

I know what people think about celebrity restaurants: a celebrity puts their name on it, and in a year it's out of business. Not for me. Trejo's Tacos isn't a vanity project. It's a love letter to L.A. When we opened our first location on La Brea, the lines

wrapped around the block. It was like Pink's Hot Dogs but with tacos—and in a town that probably has more taco joints than any city outside of Mexico. People say, "What's your secret to success?" and I tell them, "It's no secret . . . it's just good food!"

There are some days when I wake up and I don't feel like this is real. I think somebody's gonna shake me awake saying, "Hey, Danny, wake up. It's time to go to chow." And I'm going to look around and still be in prison. But instead every day I wake up and pray to do a good job, help someone, take good selfies with fans, go to the restaurant and make sure everybody's getting the taco they want. I'm living the dream. I've said this before: Every good thing that's ever happened to me is a direct result of me helping somebody else. Like I said, it's not where you start, it's where you finish. And, you know what? At Trejo's Tacos we're only getting started.

MIX IT MEXICAN

I wish I'd had the book you're holding in your hands twenty years ago. It would've made my life a lot easier. But back then it wouldn't have been possible. There wasn't a modern Mexican food revolution happening across the country—there was no such thing as a vegan cauliflower taco! Now there are hundreds of Mexican cookbooks that claim to offer the most authentic, regional, cheffy, easy, technique-driven, healthy, mind-blowing recipes out there. My book is none of those things. It's a crazy mash-up of the sometimes healthy, Mexican-adjacent, vegan-ish, always delicious food we serve at Trejo's.

I was a single dad for a while and used to cook for my kids. But if I'm going to be honest, I have to admit it was all a bit of an act. One of my tricks was to buy Hungry Jack pancake mix (you know, the "just add water" stuff that comes in a box), sit my kids down in the dining room, and then call out from the kitchen, "Okay kids, I'm making pancakes!" They'd be sitting in the other room and couldn't see me, so I'd go to the door and throw flour up in the air and they'd see it fly out the door—and I'd pop my head out and say, "Okay, wait," and then I'd throw a pan to make a noise like "Don't worry, I'm working in here." Finally I'd come out with a stack of pancakes this big (imagine my hands spread really far apart) and the kids would say, "Whoa, Dad just made the best pancakes!" Until they found the box, I had my kids believing I even churned the butter.

I'm the same way today. I like to cook when I can, but in reality, my work schedule doesn't give me much time. Luckily, Trejo's Tacos has a super-talented team of chefs who have put together a menu that celebrates all the great flavors of homemade Mexican food. Sometimes when I feel like cooking I'll drop into the kitchen at one of the Trejo's and whip up chicken quesadillas or carne asada tacos with whatever looks good. This is how we want you to approach this book. With foundations like a good piece of marinated meat or a homemade salsa at the ready, you can build whatever you want—a burrito, a taco, a bowl, a quesadilla. Cooking this way is a little like acting: sometimes you need to stick to the script and sometimes you can improvise. This is a cookbook that lets you do both.

Back in the day, maybe there was a Mexican *abuela* cooking all day long at home, turning out those elaborate feasts like my mom did while my dad, who wore the pants in the family, went to work. Well, these days everyone wears the pants, which is good! But it also means everybody has less time. So I don't expect you to spend all day in the kitchen the way my mom did, or the way the cooks at our restaurants do. You can mix it up. Make the pork that goes in our carnitas and have it with rice. Cook up some black beans and rice, make *pico de gallo*, and you've got dinner. Or mix store-bought salsa with a braised meat and some leftover rice from Chinese takeout—it will be delicious. We're going to give you our recipes just as we prepare them, and yes, some of them have a lot of steps because we believe in putting in the time to build layers of flavor. But you don't have to cook every single component each time if you don't feel like it. Look at a recipe and cook it the way it makes sense for you and your life.

This is the spirit of my restaurants and my taco trucks in cookbook form. Have what you want your way. You want healthy? Go vegan. You want a rich and boldly spiced burrito with a margarita? We've got you covered. You are free to do with it as you will. I might tell you to use a particular salsa with a certain taco, but you should do whatever the hell you want and put the cashew crema on the brown rice if you feel like it, or don't use the pickled onions if you hate tanginess.

So don't think of the recipes as being a strict guide, but also don't go totally crazy either. You're not going to put the diablo sauce on the rice pudding. Okay, maybe you could. Who am I to say? We're the people who made a donut that tastes like nachos, with jalapeños and hot sauce and cheddar cheese. It's savory and it is delicious. We broke a rule and it worked. You can, too. Maybe you'll start a whole new spicy rice pudding trend!

I'm also sharing secrets from the restaurants so you can learn how my team thinks and works behind the scenes. There's a method to this madness. It's a suggested set of actions, and tools, and techniques that you can play with. We don't expect you to think like a professional chef, but it doesn't hurt to pay attention to the principles behind the way all of this works. We pair contrasting flavors and textures to make something taste good so you want to take bite after bite without it being boring

or too heavy, too rich, or too spicy. It's that simple. Whether it's a dinner for you and your family, a quinceañera, a backyard barbecue, or a healthy lunch, there's something in this cookbook for you.

Before I owned the restaurants, I loved good food, but I wasn't what you'd call a "foodie." I knew what I liked but I couldn't tell you precisely why. Working with the team of chefs at Trejo's, I've picked up some foodie knowledge and terms along the way. And now I realize I knew more than I thought.

Take guacamole. It's all about contrasting flavors and textures. Okay, a ripe avocado is already pretty delicious because it's rich and savory and fatty. On its own you can have maybe a bite. Do you want ten bites of it? No. It's too rich and, honestly, a little boring. Put some salt on it and it boosts the flavor in a way that's sort of sweet when you think about it. Now add a squeeze of lime. There you go: it's even more interesting. It's tangy now, but still rich and kind of salty-sweet. Throw in some tortilla chips to scoop it up with and you add crunch and a different sort of sweetness from the corn in the chips, plus another hit of salty. Now you can have the ten bites and you're at the bottom of the bowl! Think that's deep? That's just plain guacamole. To my version, we add pistachios (toasty, crunchy, salty, earthy), serranos or jalapeños (spicy, tangy, assertive), and chopped onions (pungent and sharp). Now that's *really* deep guacamole! Every taco, burrito, entrée, quesadilla, and bowl is composed the same way: sweet tortilla, savory flavorful protein, fresh salsa, crunchy herby garnish. Over and over again. Look at me sounding like I know what I'm talking about. That's thanks to my team.

Pacoima's Art Revolution
Artist:
Lévi Ponce
ASSISTANTS:
P@H
KRISTY SA

TREJO'S PANTRY

Essential Ingredients for Making the Most of This Book

I'm known as being a pretty direct guy and I like my food to be direct with me. Like, it should be named what it is. *Carne asada* means "cooked meat." I like that. It says what it is. I like to keep things straightforward at Trejo's, too, so you always know what you're getting: real food, fresh ingredients, nothing processed. So when I'm going to go for the citrus, it's the actual lime, instead of that juice in the little plastic lime-shaped bottle. And we use a lot of limes at Trejo's, from the salsas to the marinades to the margaritas. We use fresh cilantro and spices and never the mystery "fajita seasoning" from a jar. You won't find lard in our beans — just water and beans. I want things to taste good and clean. I think a lot of people are like me — they eat healthy when they can and indulge when they feel like it. To get your food to taste its best, it's important to start with the freshest ingredients. We work with the freshest seasonal produce and bold spices, herbs, and chiles that have high impact.

In L.A. we're spoiled by all of the farm-fresh vegetables and specialty food shops. You can find everything in this town, from farmer's markets selling heritage meats and heirloom vegetables to old-school *carnicerias* and *mercados* in Latino neighborhoods. You can buy oxtail and other affordable cuts as well as every kind of fresh and dried chile imaginable.

At Trejo's we don't use anything you can't get at even the most basic grocery store: cumin, tomatoes, cilantro, jalapeños, onions, garlic. These are the building blocks of Mexican food, which we turn to over and over again at the restaurant and in the recipes in this book. We've included information on our favorite brands, how to find the best meat and vegetables, and how to make the most of them.

The SPICE CABINET

These are not exotic ingredients by any means, but they bear a little attention because they show up again and again. You may know what they are, but understanding why they work adds to your ability to cook well or even riff on our recipes as you see fit. It's sort of like customizing your classic car: just because it came with certain tires or paint job or carburetor, it doesn't mean you can't modify it to fit your taste. But you do need to understand the why and the how of it.

Dried spices are great because they keep a long time and you can simply open a few jars and add a ton of flavor to whatever you're cooking. But the fact that they're shelf-stable doesn't mean you can keep them forever. Most ground dried spices lose significant flavor after six months, so be sure to refresh your supply on a regular basis. Whole spices, like cumin and coriander seeds and whole peppercorns, can last up to a year. You will have to grind them before using them (either with a mortar and pestle or in a spice grinder), but you'll notice a difference in intensity compared to the pre-ground versions. Storing spices in a cupboard or drawer away from heat and light will extend their life.

BLACK PEPPER

Never ever buy the pre-ground black pepper. It's a far cry from whole peppercorns, which have complex flavors that can be, yes, peppery, but also lemon-like and even floral. Yes, you should have a pepper grinder, but even if you don't, just smashing and grinding some peppercorns under the bottom

of a heavy pot will result in a rough grind with a ton of flavor. Some people who like spicier, bolder flavors prefer this technique to using a grinder.

HOW TO USE IT Pre-season meats, vegetables, and sauces with freshly ground pepper before cooking to build a base layer of subtle heat.

CORIANDER

Whole coriander seeds come from the cilantro plant and have orange-y, earthy, peppery flavors that go well with pork, chicken, and fish dishes. A little goes a long way but can add a whole other layer of complexity to your cooking.

HOW TO USE IT Toast in a pan, grind up, and use as a secret ingredient in carnitas or sautéed fish dishes.

CUMIN

Most marinades and sauces served at Trejo's count on this musky, earthy, sweet, and savory spice. Some of our recipes call for pre-ground cumin for convenience and for times when we don't want the flavor to be too dominant. Other recipes call for cumin seeds, which have more oil in them, therefore more flavor, and will have a stronger presence and will add texture to the dish.

If you buy only one kind of cumin, make it the seeds, which you can always toast in a pan and then grind up to make incredibly smoky toasted cumin powder.

HOW TO USE IT Adds an earthy, sweet, and deep flavor to meats and sauces.

FRESH OR DRIED OREGANO

We use Mexican oregano instead of the more widely available Mediterranean version. Mediterranean oregano is sweet and even a little licorice-y, whereas Mexican oregano is floral, citrusy, and grassy. If you can't find Mexican oregano, feel free to use Mediterranean; we just prefer the flavor of the Mexican variety.

HOW TO USE IT To add an herbaceous note to meats and marinades.

CHILES

Chiles in all their variety of color, flavor, size, and heat are one of the great Mexican contributions to global cuisine and we use a lot of them at Trejo's, whether fresh, dried, canned, or ground.

JALAPEÑO

Of course you know this one. It's a workhorse that we pickle for escabeche and chop up fresh for our salsas, guacamole, and marinades. Every jalapeño, and every chile for that matter, has its own heat level, so taste a bit of the chile before deciding exactly how much to put in. Our recipes have baseline amounts of chile that won't overpower the dish if you're shy of spice, but feel free to dial it up or dial it down depending on your taste. For less heat, you can also halve a jalapeño lengthwise and remove the primary heat source—the seeds and ribs—before slicing or chopping it up. If a recipe calls for pickled jalapeños, feel free to use canned.

HOW TO USE IT Pickled in vinegar and sugar. Chopped fresh in bright fresh salsas. Roasted in the oven and blended into pureed salsas. Blistered on the grill or over a flame and added to salads. We even use them in our nacho cheese donuts.

FRESH SERRANO

These little torpedo-shaped green chiles pack a ton of heat and can be upwards of ten times hotter than a jalapeño. The flavor is sharp and intensely peppery and floral at the same time. Use wisely! It's tougher (but not impossible!) to remove the seeds and ribs from the small, slender serrano—you can try doing that, if you like, for less heat.

DRIED ÁRBOL

You can buy these pointy red chiles fresh or dried. At the restaurant we use dried, which intensifies the sweet side of the chile but doesn't tame the heat.

HOW TO USE IT Toast the dried chiles in a pan set over medium-low heat until they are fragrant, about 3 minutes. Set aside until they cool and turn brittle, then chop them up and you have the Mexican version of standard supermarket chile flakes. We like to add dried árbol flakes to spice rubs for meats. You can also leave them whole, soak them in hot water for 20 minutes or until they become tender, and then puree in sauces and salsas.

FRESH POBLANO

These large, moderately spicy chiles have a deep, sweet heat that comes out when they are roasted over an open flame.

HOW TO USE IT Roasted and pureed into salsas, chopped raw in fresh salsas, roasted and mixed into our cheesy mashed potatoes.

GROUND CHIPOTLE CHILE

Chipotle powder is made from jalapeños that have ripened until they're red, then dried, smoked, and ground up fine. The result is deeply flavored, almost sweet, hot, and smoky, kind of like bacon. It's so good, it's no wonder they named a chain of pseudo Mexican restaurants after it.

HOW TO USE IT For a sweet smoky heat in dry rubs.

CANNED CHIPOTLE IN ADOBO SAUCE

Canned chipotles are smoke-dried red jalapeños that have been stewed in a sweet, spicy, tangy sauce of tomatoes, garlic, onion, and vinegar. These chipotles can have a powerful spicy heat that really packs a punch. The chiles themselves can be chopped up and added to sour cream along with their flavorful sauce. It's a super-fast and multifaceted sauce to top a taco.

But be forewarned: canned chipotles are super-spicy, so a little goes a long way.

HOW TO USE IT For adding instant heat and depth of flavor to sauces and salsas.

BEANS *and* RICE

CANNED BEANS

There's no shame in using canned beans. Just rinse them under running water to remove the slimy canning liquid and then drain them well.

HOW TO USE IT They're pre-cooked, so you can mix them straight into salads or heat them up on the stove and mash them for our refried black beans.

DRIED BEANS

There's no question: cooking dried beans is way cheaper than using canned—and the flavor and texture are a whole lot better as well. You can infuse them with flavor if you cook them with aromatic vegetables like carrot, celery, onion, chile, and garlic. If you've got some time on the weekend, make a big pot of black, pinto, or red beans (page 170). You can also use small pinquito beans, which are the foundation of traditional Santa Maria barbecue up north on the central coast of California. They cook up tender and a bit faster than dried black beans.

Rancho Gordo is the country's best dried bean distributor; they supply lots of restaurants with super-fresh dried beans. Yes, dried beans can be fresh or stale, and these guys even stamp a use-by date on their batches. Look at a bag of beans—if they're shriveled and seem to be dry, don't buy them. You can cook a stale bean for hours and it will never fully tenderize.

RICE

We prefer California-grown varieties because rice grown in other parts of the world can contain higher levels of arsenic, which is a natural component of soil but can be more concentrated in imported rice. Brown rice has the most nutritional content, but some people just don't like its chewy texture and slightly nutty flavor. If that's you, that's fine—go with long-grain white rice and or white basmati rice.

Because we're always layering flavors at the restaurant, we present some rice recipes in this book that are a little more involved than the instructions you see on a box or bag of rice. If you're pressed for time, go ahead and just substitute plain white or brown rice—even takeout Chinese rice works!

OIL

You're cooking Mexican food, not Italian, so lay off the extra-virgin olive oil unless we call for it! In our kitchen, the more neutral the oil, the better. While extra-virgin olive oil has become the go-to oil for many restaurants and home cooks, we use neutral oils to allow the other ingredients and flavors to shine through. We like canola for neutral flavor and richness. If you see olive oil in one of our recipes (and we do use it when we want that bit of briny, rich, buttery flavor), take note that it's not extra-virgin most of the time. Pure olive oil has a more mellow flavor and will work just fine—and save you money, too. Just don't use in a high heat situation where it will tend to smoke.

SALT

Not all salt is created equal, with the size and shape of the crystals differing from type to type and brand to brand. We developed and tested these recipes with Diamond Crystal kosher salt and highly recommend you use that when cooking: it's the least salty of salts, which makes it harder to accidentally over-season your food. If you can't find Diamond, use table salt but cut the amount in half. Use the same formula if you're using Morton's kosher salt, which is also much saltier than Diamond.

BUTCHER BASICS
Why Meat Matters (and Seafood, Too)

My mom used to make club steak. It wasn't fancy—it was the best cut we could afford. My mom would season it, marinate it, and add so much flavor to it, it was like magic. Growing up, I didn't know what a filet was. The club steak I remember was just this cheap cut, the polar opposite of "prime," but it was delicious because of the love and care that went into cooking it. Even now, when I order a steak, rather than giving a temperature, I'll say that I want it "juicy" because Mom's club steak was always so juicy, so satisfying, and so perfect.

While steakhouses are in the business of serving up expensive prime cuts, grilled, thickly sliced, and served with a baked potato, Mexican food is about making the most of relatively affordable cuts. These are pieces of meat that start out tough but through marinating, spicing, brining, and braising, they are transformed from tough to tender, yielding flavorful, juicy results that punch through the layers of salsas and garnishes that make up the rest of the Mexican table. Think about it: a steakhouse steak is salty, juicy, and beefy, and you probably get something starchy and a simple salad on the side. A carne asada taco has so much more going on: the sweetness of a corn tortilla, the tangy sweet-and-sour crunch of pickled onions, crisp diced white onions, sweet and tart fresh *pico de gallo* with just a hint of jalapeño heat and a kiss of lime. Oh yeah, and that meat: juicy, charred, smoky with earthy-musky cumin and deep, spicy árbol chile. That's the alchemy of Mexican food: taking simple ingredients and really making them special.

Here are a few of the meats and seafood you'll find in this book.

BEEF

BRISKET

This is one of the toughest cuts of meat on the cow. It's basically the pectoralis muscle and holds most of the cow's weight. It's an impressive hunk of muscle, usually around 5 to 7 pounds, with hundreds of parallel lines of connective tissue running through it that will make it super-chewy if you cook it wrong—and insanely tender if you cook it right. Meaning: over super-low heat for 6 or more hours

meat." *Carne asada* has come to be the term used to describe the cut of meat as well, otherwise known as flank steak. Like brisket, the flank is lined with connective tissue and fat, but it's fairly thin and cooks up quickly with a hit on the grill or in a pan. The trick to making it tender is to marinate it, and also, after cooking, to slice the meat across the grain of the connective tissue. This creates lots of short strands of juiciness in every bite (if you slice it parallel to the grain, it'll be tough to chew). If you can't find flank steak, you can also use flap steak or a London broil in a similar way.

HOW TO USE IT A super-convenient last-minute steak to cook up at a barbecue or on a weeknight. Season with a little salt and pepper, finish with lime juice, and serve with pico de gallo or jarred salsa.

BONE-IN RIB EYE

This is not a typical cut in the Mexican kitchen, but sometimes we act like a steakhouse at Trejo's Cantina and put a bone-in rib eye on the menu. You can serve it with Trejo's Steak Sauce (page 54) which we'd put up against a bottle of A.1. any day. Rib eye is the opposite of a humble cut, meaning it's tender only if you cook it quickly over high heat and with great care. Getting it to that perfectly juicy medium-rare or medium is all about the timing. You want a crust on the surface of the steak, you want char, but you also want the inside to be juicy and tender.

When you're at the grocery store, look for the thickest cut you can find or have the butcher cut it for you. We like a $1\frac{1}{2}$-inch-thick steak, which gives you enough meat to allow it to get a good sear without overcooking inside. While a rib eye isn't riddled with connective tissue like a brisket or a flank, it should be well marbled with fat, meaning you want what's technically called intermuscular fat running throughout it. When you buy it, look for lots of tiny white lines of fat evenly dispersed throughout the

to allow all that connective tissue in every square inch to melt, making for some of the tenderest, juiciest, and most deliciously beefy eating there is. At Trejo's we go one extra and before we cook it, we cure it for 24 hours in a salt and sugar rub spiked with cumin, garlic, and chiles. The result is spectacular. The meat is very adaptable and can go in any one of our dishes: It makes a killer taco with just some pickled onions and not much else. It goes in our bowls and our burritos. You could even put it on a hot dog bun and it would be amazing.

HOW TO USE IT Brisket is a cut to cook when you've got time, like over a weekend. This is not a spur-of-the-moment meat. But it makes a lot, so you can cook it in advance of a big party and feed a crowd without much last-minute work.

CARNE ASADA

You don't need to be a fluent Spanish speaker to figure out this literally means simply "grilled meat. If the rib eye doesn't have good fat, look to other cuts that do, like a New York strip or boneless rib eye. These are going to work well and taste great.

HOW TO USE IT When you cook a nice steak, whether in a pan or on the grill, you want it to be close to room temperature so it will cook evenly and quickly. If it's cold straight from the refrigerator, it takes longer for the steak to warm up—and while it's warming up, it can overcook and potentially not even develop a nicely browned crust. To avoid this, take the steak out of the refrigerator at least a half hour before you're going to cook it and season it well with kosher salt on both sides. This will allow the salt to penetrate the meat as it warms up to room temp. Right before cooking it in a super-hot pan (we like to heat a heavy skillet—cast iron works great—for 5 minutes to get it blazing hot before adding the steak), blot the steak dry with paper towels and lightly salt it again. Removing the surface moisture is key to getting a good crust and making the meat even more flavorful. And these days one big piece of meat to serve one person isn't considered the healthiest way of eating, so buy a massive steak, cook it with care, carve it into ½-inch-thick slices perpendicular to the bone, place it on a platter, and serve it family-style.

GROUND BEEF

At the supermarket look for 80/20 ground beef, which is to say that the composition includes 20 percent fat. Fat is flavor, and this proportion is going to guarantee juiciness when you're making "gringo tacos" or our cheeseburger burrito or taco. Some supermarkets sell 80/20 beef marked as "butcher's trim" or "market trim." If you see this, buy it. This is typically made in-house from extra meat they have left over from trimming down more expensive and flavorful cuts like rib eye, New York strip, and short rib. It's usually the same price as or cheaper than the other ground beef in the display case.

HOW TO USE IT There's nothing more nostalgically Mexican American than a Gringo Taco (page 116) spiced with ground cumin, garlic powder, onion powder, and chili powder.

PORK *and* POULTRY

PORK SHOULDER

Sometimes called pork butt, a pork shoulder is the foundation for carnitas. Even though "pork butt" sounds like it's from the rear, it's actually part of the shoulder and has more fat than the lower part of the shoulder (which is sometimes called the picnic roast). For the juiciest, richest results, try to get the butt, though the lower shoulder will work as well.

Just like brisket, slow and low is the way to go with this cut to allow the fats and collagens to break down; the longer you cook it, the more tender it will get. Some people like to cook it overnight at 250°F to get it as ridiculously tender, wobbly, and unctuous as possible—I mean meat so soft you could eat it with a spoon. If you want to go that route, you can, but it's by no means necessary. We know you don't have all the time in the world, so our recipe for carnitas takes only 2½ hours on the stove top. It's much more manageable time-wise and it's still tender enough. But every cut of meat is different, so after 2½ hours, if you find the meat's a little tough, let it go another half hour or so. It eventually will get soft enough to pull apart.

HOW TO USE IT Heck, you can do anything with this, from making tacos, obviously, to serving the shredded pork with scrambled eggs or on a *torta*. You don't even have to keep it in the Mexican realm: with some ham, cheese, and pickles you can use it to make a mean Cuban sandwich.

CHICKEN

We make our grilled chicken with boneless chicken thighs. Not only are they a great substitute and are cheaper than chicken breast, the higher fat content means you're less likely to overcook them. Plus when you're making fried chicken, the fat on the inside can keep the pieces warm for up to half an hour after cooking, which is a nice bonus. If you are trying to eat lean, the recipes in this book work just as well with boneless chicken breasts.

SEAFOOD

FISH

Our go-to fish at the restaurant is Pacific cod: it's firm-fleshed, mild-tasting, and sustainable. It's what we beer-batter and fry for our fish tacos, but it also is great simply seared and loaded onto a tortilla with a squeeze of lime and some pico de gallo. For our blackened salmon dishes look for wild-caught salmon, which is in season in the summer. Otherwise use sustainably farmed salmon. The surest tests of freshness are the smell and firmness of the fish. You want fish that smells fresh and not fishy, and that springs back to shape if you press it with your finger. If it's a little mushy, don't buy it.

SHRIMP

Wild Gulf shrimp from Mexico is the ideal variety to buy—yes, they are more expensive than farmed shrimp from Southeast Asia, but their flavor is sweeter and cleaner.

PRODUCE

Honestly, if you have tomatoes, onions, cilantro, and jalapeños in your kitchen, you're halfway to a Mexican meal.

TOMATOES

Fact: the reason our Pico de Gallo is so damned good is that we make it with Southern California tomatoes. Yes, we're spoiled here with our long growing season and sweet, ripe tomatoes that are available nearly year-round. That said, hothouse and imported tomatoes can do the trick if you use the right ones. The medium-sized vine-ripened tomatoes that come with the stems and leaves attached are much more flavorful than the larger, paler pinkish tomatoes, and are actually pretty good if you're making a fresh salsa or roasting them for a cooked and pureed salsa. Hydroponically grown tomatoes and Roma plum tomatoes are also totally fine. Cherry tomatoes are the best out-of-season tomato to use: their small size makes them a pain to cut up, but their high-sugar/low-water content makes them by far the sweetest variety in the market.

ONIONS

Onions are critical in the Mexican kitchen—all onions, all colors. Here's how to know which onion to use when: White onions are the sharpest and most pungent onion, which you could even say have a little heat to them. When you're making Pico de Gallo, these punch through. They mellow when you cook them but still have a strong oniony taste. Yellow onions have a good balance between sweetness and strength. These are the utility player of onions and are good both raw and cooked. Red onions are the mildest and sweetest and play nicely with ingredients in salads. Using half white onions and half red onions can make Pico de Gallo a little more interesting in both flavor and color. Scallions are milder than other onions, and are a nice substitute for white onions as a taco topping.

TORTILLAS

It's getting easier and easier to find great corn tortillas in markets across the country. We get ours from a local *tortilleria* that makes its own masa. The result is tender, fresh, thick tortillas that have more flavor than most supermarket brands. Try to look for the thickest corn tortillas you can find—they won't fall apart when loaded with fillings and salsa. And if they are made from organic corn, even better. We use 6-inch tortillas so you can fill up on two or three, whereas many stands that sell cheap tacos around the city use 4-inch tortillas, which you can easily eat four or five of. Unless you're at a Texan or Sonoran taco joint, in L.A. the vast majority of tacos are made with corn tortillas (bonus: that makes most tacos here gluten-free!). We use flour tortillas for quesadillas and to wrap our burritos.

The trick to getting the most flavor from any tortilla is taking off some of that raw flavor and refrigerator chill before serving them. All they need is 15 seconds in a hot cast-iron skillet to warm them up so they become pliable and soft. If you're serving a crowd, wrap a stack of tortillas in aluminum foil and place them in a 300°F oven for 15 minutes to warm up. But be careful not to let them sit wrapped in the foil for too long because the steam will make them fall apart. A safer bet, if you have the time, is to give them 30 to 45 minutes in a 225°F oven. They'll be warm but won't be in as much danger of over-steaming.

FROM MACHETES
to MOLCAJETES
The Gear You Need

If you've got a heat source, any old pan, and a decent knife, you're going to be able to make nearly every dish in this book. But if you're planning on cooking big feasts, blitzing up lovingly roasted salsas, and refining your cooking skills as you make your way through the recipes, you're going to want some good gear. Here's a wish list of the top tools for cooking the Trejo way.

A MACHETE (OR AN 8-INCH KNIFE)

Okay, you don't actually need something as big as a machete, but you do want a big sharp knife. It's where all great cooking begins. It's the object that stands between a pile of raw produce or meat and dinner. You take that knife out and it's the heroic, symbolic beginning of a culinary victory. Cooking is work, with time and labor involved. Getting to the end of a meal efficiently and gracefully requires a tool that will become an extension of your hand.

An 8-inch stainless-steel chef's knife is the way to go. It's big enough that you can slice through bunches of cilantro, dice tomatoes evenly, devein chile peppers like a surgeon, and slice hunks of meat to just the right size. You want a knife made from stainless-steel because it keeps its edge longer than other metals. There's a saying that a sharp knife is a safer knife—that's because it'll go where you want it to without slipping. A sharp knife glides through citrus and tomatoes without sliding off the skin and possibly hitting your finger instead. You should sharpen your knives when you notice that they're starting to

dull—some chefs will sharpen theirs once a week! For a home cook, that's going overboard. In between uses, you can simply hone your knife on a sharpening steel. This realigns the edge of the blade and helps make the slicing process smoother and cleaner.

Over time you can build up a nice knife collection. In addition to that big chef's knife, you can eventually get a few others in smaller sizes—for example, a paring knife and another utility knife so you don't have to clean each knife when you're prepping separate ingredients. The head chefs at Trejo's take pride in their personal collections of knives and show up at work each day with a carrying case containing the blades they rely on. I still rely on my machete.

A GOOD HEAVY PAN

The trick to a good sear is a screaming-hot pan. At the restaurant we run our griddles at 500°F, which is hotter than most home cooks ever go with their pans. We can do this because we have high-powered commercial ventilation systems. If you heated your cast-iron skillet or oil-coated stainless-steel pan to 500°F, you'd need to open your windows wide, crank up your vent hood to full blast, and unplug your smoke detector! You don't have to go as far as we do, but you do need to let your pan get as hot as it can handle when you're searing meat. That means gas at full bore or electric at blazing hot.

The quality of a good pan is all about the metal. First of all, it should be on the heavy side. "Heavy" means more metal, and that means it will heat more evenly. A thin pan will have hot spots that will burn meat in some spots while it undercooks it in others. Cast iron is great to cook with, but some people find it too heavy to maneuver and tough to clean. Stainless-steel pans with an aluminum core conduct heat well and are easier to clean. Nonstick pans are good for cooking eggs and fish, which tend to stick to other surfaces, but you don't want to do much high-heat searing in them because it can damage the coating. A good pan can be expensive, but it doesn't need to be. You can get a cast-iron pan with an old soul and a thick bottom at a yard sale. This is what's going to give your asada good color, and your steak good crust.

A DEEP POT

If you're going to be doing any of the fried dishes, like the beer-battered fish tacos (page 108) or the donuts on page 183 (you *have* to make the donuts!), you're going to need a pot that is deep enough to easily hold several cups of oil for frying. You need a lot of oil to keep the temperature consistent when you add the food, and it's safer to have high sides so the oil doesn't bubble over. A deep pot comes in handy for making soup and for boiling pasta, so even if you fry only a few times a year, a nice tall pot is a good item to have. And if you're not going to be searing meat in it, go for a lighter-gauge, more affordable model.

AN INSTANT-READ THERMOMETER

There's no point in guessing what the internal temperature of a piece of meat is—not when, for around 15 bucks, you can get an instant-read thermometer that will save you from rubbery when you wanted rare. Invest in this to keep your meat bills down.

A MOLCAJETE

It's the original mortar and pestle—the prehistoric blender. But instead of a glass pitcher with a rotating blade, there's a big bowl made of lava with a matching stubby cylinder designed for mashing. You can use it to grind up spices, to transform chiles, garlic, and herbs into pastes, and to make marinades, salsas, and guacamole. It's more labor-intensive than using a blender or food processor, but it yields a chunkier, more rustic product. My mother preferred the molcajete, and in many Latin families it becomes a treasured heirloom.

A HIGH-POWERED BLENDER

At the other end of the technological spectrum from the molcajete sits the high-powered blender. At Trejo's we use Vitamix blenders to puree sauces, table salsas, and marinades. These are pretty much the industry standard when it comes to blending. The thing is so powerful that if you leave it running too long, the blades will heat the mixture up and actually cook the contents. The great thing about a high-powered blender is that you can make big batches of special sauces and salsas. Home cooks can make gifts for friends or enough marinade to store or freeze for later.

A LIME JUICER

Some of the recipes in this book rely on large quantities of fresh lime juice. To make the ceviche, for example, you'll need 2 cups. If you're going to make margaritas for a party, by the end of the night you might've gone through 4 cups of lime juice. That's a lot of juicing. While you can definitely squeeze limes by hand, a hinged aluminum juicer or an electric juicer is affordable and compact, and can help make large quantities quickly.

A STAND MIXER

Working donut and churro doughs requires some muscle. A heavy-duty stand mixer with a powerful motor and multiple attachments is crucial if you're a big baker.

PASADENA

DOWNTOWN

Trejo Town

A (Mostly) Food-Focused Look at Danny's L.A.

Like Randy Newman says, I love L.A. But I think my L.A. is a little different than his. From Baldwin Park all the way to Compton and Watts, to the Northern Valley and Boyle Heights and Montebello, I've been all over this vast and diverse city in my seventy-plus years of living here. I've seen a lot of it change, but to me so much that I love has stayed the same. It's the best place on the face of the planet because it has everything.

L.A. is like a massive sprawling puzzle with little pieces of this and that that come and go. Don't think about completing the puzzle—it's never going to happen, because the puzzle keeps changing. Take the sports teams: my favorite football team, the Rams, was here when I was a kid, moved to St. Louis for a while, and then came back four years ago and made it to the Super Bowl! This town was once full of Chevy Impalas and Dodge Darts, and now they've been replaced by Teslas and Priuses, and that's a good thing because we don't have the smog problem the way we used to. But I still like to tinker with my old cars in my driveway. I like oldie's, Soul, and R & B, but I also produce rap. The restaurants come and go, but the really good ones stay in business and those are the ones I tend to like: Musso & Frank, Du-par's, The Pantry.

Guys still work out on Venice Beach like I did in the '70s, and you can still find the best taquitos at Cielito Lindo on Olvera Street, near the old Spanish Mission, where they also sell churros that are almost as good as the ones we serve. The rickety old funicular railway Angels Flight still runs up Bunker Hill, but a lot of people don't remember that it used to be half a block up the street. People also don't realize that the first In-N-Out Burger was in Baldwin Park in the San Gabriel Valley. I've been eating In-N-Out for a long time (double-double protein style, if you're wondering). Now Trejo's Tacos is adding more pieces to the puzzle.

I don't need to tell you to go see Grauman's Chinese Theatre or the Santa Monica Pier or Disney Hall—but my favorite spots are a little more off the beaten path, and I'd really like you to visit them to get a real taste of old L.A. These are a few of my favorite places—joints I hung out in, helped build, have been eating at for decades, acted in, and get my cars worked on (because everyone needs a great mechanic in this town!).

The RESTAURANTS

Now that I've got a restaurant, people are constantly asking me what my favorite restaurant is. Well, of course I answer "Trejo's Tacos." When I'm *not* eating at my own restaurants, there is a handful of dependables that I go to over and over again. They've all been around since at least the 1950s. I really hope that I'm lucky enough for Trejo's Tacos to join them as an L.A. institution and be around for another fifty years.

For me, restaurants fall into two categories: restaurants I *eat* at and restaurants I *dine* in. For example, I'll eat at the 24-hour diner Pantry but dine at Musso & Frank. The difference is the ambience, the service, the preparation, and the presentation. When the tempo is "let's go, go, go" like a diner or an old-school café, that's eating. When it's more relaxed and it's about sitting down and enjoying each other's company, we'll dine—and when I go out with my sons, Danny Boy and Gilbert, and my daughter, Danielle, that's dining at its best.

RESTAURANTS FOR EATING

THE PANTRY CAFE The waiters are fast and friendly, they only take cash, and you pay at a little teller window like at the bank. It's open 24 hours a day and has not closed its doors since it first opened in 1924. Not even when they moved locations: they opened the doors to the new one before closing the doors on the old one! This is where to come for eggs and bacon and pancakes and hot coffee and history. The fact that you can get all that for 12 bucks plus tip any hour of the day is a beautiful thing.

DU-PAR'S AT THE FARMERS MARKET The Original Farmers Market in L.A. is literally the *original* farmer's market; it opened up in 1934 before all the hipster neighborhoods in L.A. had markets selling kale and fancy heirloom tomatoes. Yes, you can buy kale at the produce stands, but you'll also find stores that specialize in hot sauce, crepes, Cajun food, specialty meats, donuts, and pancakes, and now there's a Trejo's Tacos too, which I'm incredibly proud of. Until Trejo's opened, my favorite spot was Du-par's, a classic American diner. These guys have been around since 1938 and serve the very best pancakes in all of L.A. They're fluffy, made with buttermilk, and they don't hold back on the butter.

Eating pancakes there with my best friend Eddie Bunker was at least a weekly ritual before he passed away in 2005. Eddie was the guy I owe my movie career to as much as anyone. We did time in San Quentin together. I still go to Du-par's whenever I can and it always makes me think of Eddie and how far I've come.

BOB'S BIG BOY IN BURBANK Before there were Big Boy diners all across the country, it was strictly an L.A. chain. Me and my Uncle Gilbert used to rob people in the parking lot of the one in Burbank to support our drug habit. When I was working on the Michael Mann movie *Heat* with Robert De Niro, we were shooting a scene there. A lot of the guys who work security on movie shoots are ex-cops, and one of them recognized my name and was saying to himself, "Trejo, Trejo," like he was trying to place me. So I say, "You're thinking of my Uncle Gilbert." The cop replies, "Yeah, he and you robbed this place." So finally I say, "Yeah, something like that." Sometimes people remember me from when I didn't just *play* a bad guy on the screen. Now a bunch of us get together and do a Friday-night cruise around Bob's Big Boy with our restored classic cars and lowriders. We don't eat, though—that

would require going inside! This is a place to be seen in the parking lot, showing off your cars.

LOS TRES HERMANOS While eight Trejo's Tacos seems like a lot of restaurants, it's just a drop in the bucket of all the restaurants serving Mexican food in L.A. Every single neighborhood has at least one, and sometimes twenty, Mexican restaurants, and my spot is Los Tres Hermanos. Now this is authentic L.A. Mexican food: you can get O.G. L.A. Mexican dishes like wet *lengua* burritos drenched in red sauce and drizzled with crema (if you want, you can get your burritos at Trejo's wet, too), taquitos, and every imaginable combo platter. Everybody needs a neighborhood spot and this one is mine.

A RESTAURANT FOR DINING

MUSSO & FRANK Yes, there's just one restaurant in this category because it's *the* restaurant for dining . . . and you can't get more classic old-school Hollywood than Musso's. First of all, it has been around since 1919. Musso's has seen Hollywood through the golden era, the '70s (which you could

call the tarnished era), to the renaissance happening now also. It's dripping in history: Raymond Chandler wrote about it in his noir detective novels. Charles Bukowski hung out here. It's got the red vinyl booths, the dark wood, the old waiters who've been there for thirty years wear red blazers and bow ties, and treat you like royalty. Musso's is known for their steaks that are cooked over a wood-fired grill, and if I'm in the mood for a fine steak I'll go there. But my favorite dish is the chicken pot pie. It's my standing order. They only serve it on Thursdays and always sell out—but they know me, so I make sure to call ahead and reserve a few before I go. My son Gilbert will call me and I know where we're going when he says: "Dad, it's Thursday. I've already reserved three!"

OTHER PLACES BESIDES RESTAURANTS

THE CINERAMA DOME IN HOLLYWOOD This massive domed movie theater on Sunset Boulevard is world-famous. Between stints in prison, I worked construction for a company called CD Wales and helped build the concrete forms that made up the domed ceiling. I was sent back to prison before the building was completed, and when I finally got out, it was one of the most renowned movie theaters in the world. Since then, many of my movies have been screened and premiered there. Every time I walk the red carpet there I think about how far I've come.

MUSCLE BEACH IN VENICE I used to eat a lot of meat because of this place. At Muscle Beach I'd try to keep up with my old buddy Craig Monson, who also did time in San Quentin. "Keep up" is a relative term: he weighed over 300 pounds and could bench-press 500 pounds with a wide grip! Lifting a ton of weights and eating everything in sight, I topped out at 190 pounds. When I started acting more, I realized that the camera puts on 10 pounds and I looked like I was a guy who spent all his time in the gym when I wanted to play guys who were just tough, so I dropped some weight and I got more work. Go figure.

CHUBBY'S AUTOMOTIVE Chubby's Automotive is where you will find me in my spare time, working on my cars. In my collection I've got a gleaming, chromed-out, black custom 1952 Chevy Stepside truck, a 1976 Cadillac lowrider with a hydraulic system, and a midnight-blue 1965 Riviera, and I can't stop improving them, adding a little more chrome here and there, maintaining their hydraulic systems, getting everything just right. Chubby's dad was a backyard mechanic when we were growing up, and when he opened a shop in the San Fernando Valley, Chubby followed. I store my cars at home in what I call Machete's Garage. This is my happy place where I go to relax and to reflect on my past and present life. My cars blend both together. Ha! I guess that is what you could say about the food at Trejo's. It is a combination of the food I was raised on and the healthy lifestyle I try to maintain now.

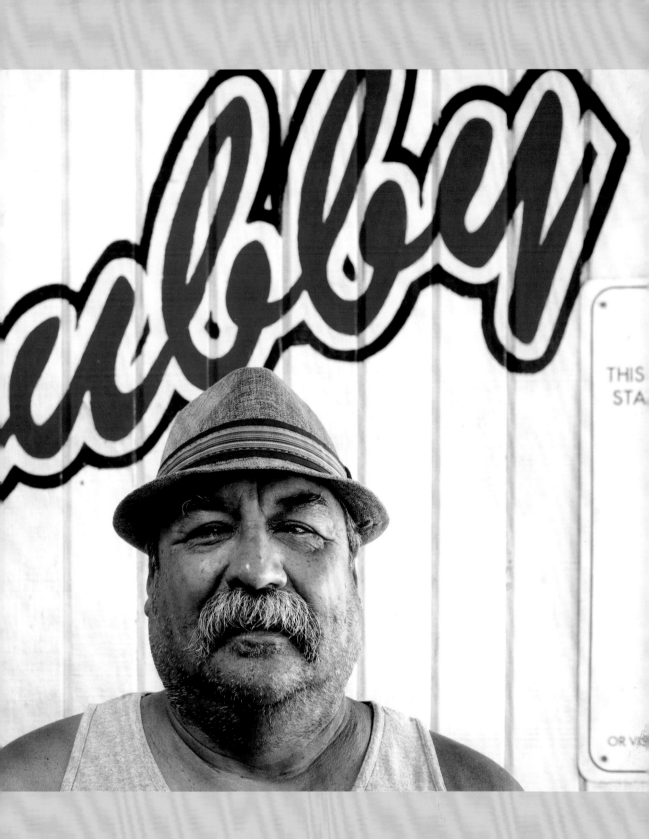

Cremas, Sauces & Vinaigrettes

Salsas, sauces, and cremas are what take our food from good to great. They can make a simple piece of grilled chicken bright and sunny or deeply smoky and spicy or sweet and tangy. Some people think of these as the finishing touches, but to us they are our secret weapons: full of flavor and most of the time very healthy. Some of these are as simple as throwing a few ingredients into a bowl and mixing it up with a spoon. Others require multiple steps like chopping and dicing and roasting and toasting and blending and pureeing. They're all worth the effort because they all make a big impact. We suggest you make the marinades and sauces in large quantities so you can save some for later in the week, freeze some to whip out a month or so down the road, or give leftovers to friends and neighbors.

We've broken these recipes out as their own section because we don't want to limit what you do with them. If you want to buy a rotisserie chicken at the supermarket and serve it with a side of our roasted tomato salsa, you're a genius. If you put our Trejo's Steak Sauce on a hamburger, we're going to ask for a bite. If you dip your French fries into our chipotle sour cream, McDonald's might steal the idea. Yes, we've thought of using the Pepita Pesto on pasta instead of on our brisket. And no, you don't have to restrict yourself to using the chipotle-spiked diablo sauce only for shrimp. You can use it on tofu, seitan, or Tofurkey if you want to—with a great marinade or sauce, you can really transform just about anything.

Crema and salsa are like good cop/bad cop: one plays it hot and in your face (salsa), while the other plays it cool and soothing (crema—unless it's the chipotle crema, which goes both ways). *Crema* is Spanish for "cream"; we mix ours with spices, chiles, and citrus juice and use it to top tacos and bowls and to sauce our burritos. Cremas are the underutilized, unsung sauce of the Mexican kitchen and we think they basically belong on everything. Throughout this book, we pair specific cremas with their perfect taco partner, but they're good enough to mix and match as you wish.

And here's an incredible fact: Apart from the cremas, every single one of the recipes in this section is 100 percent vegan (and we do offer a Vegan Cashew Crema on page 59); there's no butter or lard—nothing to mask the vibrancy and potency of the marinade, salsa, or sauce. This food was born to be delicious first and foremost—being healthy is a happy coincidence!

PICO DE GALLO

You don't even need to know how to cook to make this salsa. All you need to know is how to chop (sure, you could use a machete, but a sharp chef's knife is better!). If you're going to buy store-bought sauces and salsas to substitute in some of the dishes in this book, I won't be mad. But once you make fresh pico de gallo—a simple combination of chopped ripe tomatoes, cilantro, onion, jalapeño, and fresh lime juice—the prepared stuff at the supermarket will be a letdown.

In the restaurant we go through *hundreds* of gallons of pico de gallo a week. Pico is the quintessential Mexican condiment that goes with everything on our menu and that you should put on regular rotation in your household: put it on eggs with some hot sauce in the morning, serve it with simple rice and beans, or top a piece of seared fish.

While we give measurements here, they're honestly just a suggestion; any good *abuela* or *taquero* would make it their own. Once you've made this a few times, you won't even need to use a recipe anymore. The point is you want mostly tomatoes, fewer onions, less cilantro, and a hit of chile, lime, and salt. Play with the amounts and make it the way you want—if you want even coverage of your chips and tacos, chop everything into a meticulous quarter-inch dice. If you're in a rush, go bigger. There are no strict rules.

Makes about 3 cups

2 ripe medium tomatoes, cored and diced

½ small red onion, diced

½ small white onion, diced

2 jalapeños, halved, seeds and ribs removed, diced

¼ cup chopped fresh cilantro

Juice of 1 lime

1 tablespoon pure olive oil

1 teaspoon kosher salt

Add the tomatoes, onions, jalapeños, cilantro, lime juice, olive oil, and salt to a medium bowl and mix well. Now taste it. Does it need more salt or acid? If so, add a pinch or two of salt (add a little at first—you can always add more, but you can't take it away) or a squeeze of lime juice. When it tastes the way you want it to, you're done.

Trejo's Tips

FINDING JUICY TOMATOES

Farmer's markets in L.A. are a thing of beauty, and just about every neighborhood has one, from Santa Monica, where the chefs hang out, to Hollywood, where the celebrities buy their kale.

In California we're spoiled with beautiful weather year-round that helps bring forward the juiciest and sweetest tomatoes on the planet. Pretty much anywhere else in the country, unless it's the middle of summer, finding a perfect tomato is a problem. In the fall and winter the big red tomatoes at the supermarket can be bland and mealy; Romas can be pithy and firm. We've found that cherry tomatoes or those vine-ripened tomatoes still on the stems are pretty reliable for making pico de gallo and other salsas.

COMBINING ONION VARIETIES

This recipe calls for both red and white onions because they each bring a different flavor to the salsa, red being sweeter and milder, white being more pungent. The two different colors make the salsa look prettier, too. But don't sweat it if you only have one type of onion. It'll still be delicious.

PICKLED RED ONIONS

These quick-pickled onions add a tangy-sweet crunch to any dish and can help balance out the richness of heartier, richer tacos like the carnitas (page 86) or the shrimp (page 120). While the flavors mellow and taste best after a night in the fridge, you can go ahead and use the onions after an hour or so of marinating.

Makes about 2 cups

1 medium red onion, halved and thinly sliced

½ cup apple cider vinegar

1 tablespoon sugar

1½ teaspoons kosher salt

Place the onion slices in a large heat-safe bowl.

In a medium saucepan, combine ½ cup of water with the vinegar, sugar, and salt and bring to a boil over high heat. Remove from the heat and stir until the sugar and salt have dissolved. Then pour the hot liquid over the onions.

Let the liquid cool to room temperature, and then cover the bowl with plastic wrap (or transfer the onions and liquid to a pint jar) and refrigerate it overnight to allow the flavors to meld and mellow. Pickled onions can be refrigerated for up to a week.

Trejo's Tip

POWER TO THE PICKLE

There are no rules to our escabeche. Add cauliflower florets or red bell pepper if you want — make the recipe your own. Or don't — we stand by our escabeche but there's no shame in using a canned version. We like the one made by Embasa, which you can get at Latin markets and in a lot of supermarkets, either in the international foods aisle or in the pickle section.

ESCABECHE
(PICKLED JALAPEÑOS & CARROTS)

Most of the food at Trejo's is super-healthy, but sometimes Mexican food can be a little bit heavy if you're eating something smothered in cheese or tackling a large portion of rich braised meats. That's when you want something bright and fresh on your plate, like these pickled vegetables. Angelenos know these from all the taqueria salsa tables where you go right after getting your order to add the finishing touch of spicy-sour to your combo platter: you've got your red salsa, your tomatillo salsa, and your escabeche. You can add the escabeche to tacos or bowls or just eat it on the side along with chips, guacamole, and salsa.

Makes about 5 cups

- 1 tablespoon pure olive oil
- 4 jalapeños, sliced into ¼-inch-thick rounds
- 2 medium carrots, sliced into ¼-inch-thick rounds
- 1 medium white onion, sliced into ¼-inch-thick rounds
- 8 garlic cloves

- 2 teaspoons whole cumin seeds
- 2½ tablespoons kosher salt
- 2 cups apple cider vinegar
- 4 dried chiles de árbol
- 2 teaspoons dried oregano
- 1 teaspoon sugar
- ½ teaspoon whole black peppercorns

Heat the olive oil in a large skillet over medium heat until it is shimmering, about 2 minutes. Then add the jalapeños, carrots, onion, garlic, cumin, and a pinch of the salt. Cook, stirring occasionally, until the onions are translucent but not browned, 5 to 7 minutes. Remove from the heat and set aside.

In a medium saucepan set over medium heat, combine the vinegar with 2 cups of water, the chiles, salt, oregano, sugar, and peppercorns, and bring to a simmer.

Once the pickling liquid is at a simmer, add the reserved vegetables and return it to a boil. Remove the pan from the heat and set it aside to cool to room temperature.

Transfer the mixture to an airtight container and refrigerate until chilled, at least 1 hour, before serving, or store it for up to 1 week.

SALSA VERDE

We've served this as a taco topper, as a table salsa, and as a sauce for branzino and other fish specials we sometimes run at the restaurant. Cooking the whole tomatillos and jalapeño in the skillet softens the vegetables and blisters their skins, adding a deep toasty flavor to the salsa. Like our Pico de Gallo (page 48) it's very versatile . . . and very delicious.

Makes about 2 cups

- 12 medium tomatillos (about 1½ pounds), papery skin removed, tomatillos left whole
- 1 medium jalapeño, left whole
- 2 garlic cloves
- ½ medium white onion
- ¼ cup chopped fresh cilantro
- Juice of 1 lime, plus extra to taste
- 1 tablespoon kosher salt, plus extra to taste

Heat a large heavy skillet over medium heat until it is very hot, about 4 minutes. Add the whole tomatillos and jalapeño. They should sizzle when they hit the dry hot pan. Cook until the vegetables are black and blistered in spots and soft on one side, 5 to 7 minutes. Use tongs to turn the tomatillos and jalapeño over. Add the garlic cloves. Cook the tomatillos, jalapeño, and garlic until the tomatillos and jalapeño are blistered and the garlic cloves are toasted but not burned, 5 to 7 minutes more. Remove the pan from the heat and let the mixture cool to room temperature.

Transfer the tomatillos, jalapeño, and garlic to a blender or food processor and add the onion, cilantro, lime juice, and salt. Process until the sauce is completely smooth. Taste and add more salt or lime juice if desired. Transfer the sauce to a bowl and chill before serving, or refrigerate it in an airtight container for up to 5 days.

SALSA VERDE

SALSA ROJA
(ROASTED TOMATO & CHIPOTLE SALSA)

This is one of the most versatile salsas we have on the menu: you can put it on any of our tacos, put it in a bowl to serve with chips, or, honestly, just slather it on a store-bought rotisserie chicken. Roasting the vegetables caramelizes them and intensifies their natural sweetness. Smoky and spicy chipotles in adobo sauce add heat and depth of flavor.

Makes about 3 cups

- 4 tablespoons pure olive oil
- 4 medium tomatoes, cored and halved
- 4 garlic cloves
- ½ large white onion, roughly chopped
- 2 jalapeños, halved, seeds and ribs removed, diced
- 1 teaspoon kosher salt, plus extra to taste
- 1 teaspoon freshly ground black pepper
- ½ cup roughly chopped fresh cilantro
- 2 chipotle chiles from a can of chipotle chiles in adobo sauce, plus 2 tablespoons of the adobo sauce
- Juice of 1 lime, plus extra to taste

Preheat the oven to 425°F.

Evenly coat an 11 x 17-inch baking sheet with 2 tablespoons of the olive oil. Place the tomatoes, garlic, onion, and jalapeños on the baking sheet and season them with the salt and pepper. Roast the vegetables until they are soft and are charred in some spots, stirring them halfway through, 15 to 20 minutes.

Transfer the roasted vegetables to a blender. Add the cilantro, chipotle chiles, adobo sauce, and lime juice and puree until smooth. Taste and adjust the seasoning with more salt and lime juice if needed. Serve immediately or transfer to an airtight container; the salsa will keep in the refrigerator for up to 1 week.

TREJO'S STEAK SAUCE

SALSA ROJA

TREJO'S STEAK SAUCE

For a while we had a bone-in rib eye on the menu at the Cantina, as a sort of homage to the great steakhouses of L.A., like the Pacific Dining Car and Musso & Frank (see page 39). We wanted to serve it with a Mexican-ish take on the classic A.1. steak sauce, so we used guajillo chiles and agave along with the flavors packed into a bottle of A.1.: it's tangy and sweet and so good you'll want to eat it with a spoon.

Makes about 2 cups

1 medium head garlic (about 10 cloves), cloves separated and peeled

1 large red onion, roughly diced

6 dried guajillo chiles, stems and seeds removed

½ cup canola oil

Juice of 1 lime

2 tablespoons agave syrup

1 tablespoon adobo sauce from a can of chipotles in adobo (see Trejo's Tip)

2 teaspoons kosher salt, plus extra to taste

1 teaspoon chipotle chile powder

1 teaspoon ground cumin

1 teaspoon red wine vinegar

Trejo's Tip

STORING LEFTOVER CHILES

This recipe calls for just 1 tablespoon of adobo sauce, so store the leftover chiles and sauce in a plastic or glass container in your refrigerator for up to 1 week. You can also freeze the leftovers in a freezer bag for up to 2 months.

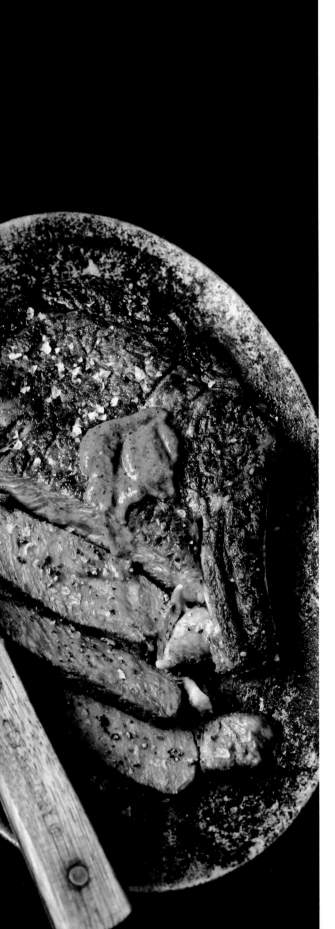

Preheat the oven to 350°F.

Spread the garlic cloves and diced onion on an 11 x 17-inch sheet pan and bake until they are golden brown and soft, about 45 minutes. Leaving the oven on, transfer the garlic and onions to a blender.

Place the guajillo chiles on the sheet pan and bake them until they are fragrant and lightly toasted, 2 to 5 minutes.

Meanwhile, in a medium saucepan, bring 4 cups of water to a low boil. Remove the pan from the heat and let the water cool for 5 minutes.

Add the chiles to the water, cover the saucepan, and set it aside for 20 minutes to let the chiles soften.

Drain the chiles and roughly chop them. Put them in the blender with the garlic and onions and add the oil, lime juice, agave, adobo sauce, salt, chile powder, cumin, and red wine vinegar. Blend until smooth, then taste and add more salt if needed. Serve immediately or refrigerate in an airtight container for up to 5 days.

PEPITA PESTO

In the spirit of zero waste of food, effort, or the funds needed to make this pesto, we encourage you to come up with new ways of using it. At the restaurant it's served as a sauce for the Carne Asada Burritos (page 83), but don't let that keep you from serving it with grilled steak or chicken, or, yes, pasta.

Makes about 1 cup

About 1½ cups roughly chopped fresh cilantro

About 2 cups roughly chopped fresh flat-leaf parsley

6 garlic cloves

1 cup unsalted raw pepitas (pumpkin seeds)

½ teaspoon kosher salt, plus extra to taste

½ cup pure olive oil

Put the cilantro and parsley in a food processor and add the garlic, pepitas, and salt. Pulse for 5 seconds and then scrape down the sides of the bowl. Repeat the pulsing and scraping about 5 more times, until the ingredients are finely minced. While the machine is running, slowly pour the olive oil through the feed tube, processing until the pesto is combined and looks like coarse meal, about 30 seconds, scraping down sides if necessary.

Taste and adjust the seasoning with more salt as needed. Use the pesto immediately or transfer it to an airtight container or glass jar (see Trejo's Tip) and refrigerate it for up to 3 days.

Trejo's Tip

HOW TO STORE PESTO

To keep pesto from oxidizing and discoloring, pour a thin layer of olive oil over the pesto after you've transferred it to a jar.

CREAMY CILANTRO-LIME VINAIGRETTE

Vegan mayonnaise gives this creamy vinaigrette the body of ranch dressing with the acidity and brightness of a vinaigrette, so you really get the best of both worlds. We use it to dress our kale salad. It would also be great on a simple green salad, served as a sauce alongside seared salmon or grilled chicken, or drizzled on any of our bowls.

Makes about 2 cups

1½ cups chopped fresh cilantro

½ cup vegenaise (Just Mayo is good, too)

Juice of 1 lime

For a creamy-smooth dressing, combine the cilantro, vegenaise, lime juice, and ¼ cup of water in a blender and puree until smooth. For a chunkier vinaigrette, combine everything in a medium bowl and whisk until emulsified (that's the fancy word for thoroughly mixed so that the juice is suspended evenly throughout the fats). Use immediately or refrigerate in an airtight container for up to 5 days.

ESCABECHE-MINT CREMA

If you happen to have some extra escabeche in your fridge, use it in this fresh and spicy crema. Otherwise, buy a can or jar of Embasa pickled jalapeños. (It's not worth cooking a whole batch of escabeche just for the 2 tablespoons needed for this recipe.) I love this with seared fish and on our chicken tikka tacos (page 91).

Makes about 1 cup

1 cup sour cream

2 tablespoons chopped pickled jalapeños or Escabeche (page 51)

Juice of 1 lime

1 tablespoon roughly chopped fresh mint leaves

1 teaspoon ground cumin

1 teaspoon kosher salt

¼ teaspoon cayenne pepper

Put the sour cream, jalapeño, lime juice, mint, cumin, salt, and cayenne in a blender and puree until smooth. Serve immediately or transfer to an airtight container and refrigerate for up to 3 days.

VEGAN CASHEW CREMA

You don't have to be vegan to love this crema. Pureed cashews are so buttery, you'll swear this is made with dairy.

Makes about 2 cups

2 cups raw unsalted cashews

Juice of 1 lime, plus extra to taste

Juice of 1 lemon, plus extra to taste

1½ teaspoons kosher salt, plus extra to taste

Place the cashews in a blender jar and cover them with 1½ cups of water. Set the cashews aside to soak for at least 2 hours or up to overnight. The longer they soak, the softer they'll get, making for a creamier result.

Pour off the water and add the lime juice, lemon juice, and salt to the cashews. Puree until creamy and smooth. Taste and adjust with more salt, lemon, and/or lime juice if needed. Use immediately or refrigerate in an airtight container for up to 5 days.

LIME CREMA

The zippy acidity in this lime crema makes it particularly good with fried food, which is why we use it to dress the slaw that goes on the fried fish tacos (page 108). Zesting the lime with a rasp-style grater (like a Microplane) will make this easy crema even easier.

Makes about 1 cup

1 cup sour cream

1 teaspoon finely chopped lime zest

Juice of 1 lime

1 teaspoon kosher salt

In a small mixing bowl, combine the sour cream, lime zest, lime juice, and salt and mix well. Serve immediately or refrigerate in an airtight container for up to 3 days.

CHIPOTLE CREMA

This is one of the easiest, most full-flavored, and most satisfying sauces in this book—and watch out, it's spicy! Play it safe; start with 4 chipotles, taste, and then add more if you think you can handle it.

Makes about 2 cups

2 cups sour cream

4 chipotle chiles from a can of chipotle chiles in adobo sauce, plus 2 tablespoons of the adobo sauce

Juice of 2 limes

2 teaspoons kosher salt

Put the sour cream, chipotles, adobo sauce, lime juice, and salt in a blender and puree until smooth. Serve immediately or transfer to an airtight container and refrigerate for up to 3 days.

CUMIN CREMA

We serve this earthy crema with our sautéed fish tacos (page 106), but it's super-versatile and would also go well with the fried fish tacos (page 108) or our chicken tikka tacos (page 91).

Makes about 1 cup

1 cup sour cream

2 tablespoons ground cumin

1 teaspoon kosher salt

In a small mixing bowl, whisk together the sour cream, cumin, and salt until well combined. Use immediately, or refrigerate in an airtight container for up to 3 days

CUMIN CREMA

CHIPOTLE CREMA

AVOCADO CREMA

Creamy avocado meets tangy sour cream in this cooling crema that you can use on any of our tacos.

Makes about 2 cups

2 medium avocados, halved, pitted, and peeled

½ cup sour cream

½ cup roughly chopped fresh cilantro

Juice of 1 lime, plus extra to taste

1 teaspoon kosher salt, plus extra to taste

Combine the avocados, sour cream, cilantro, lime juice, and salt in a blender and puree until smooth. Taste and add more salt or lime juice if desired. Use immediately or store in an airtight container for up to 3 days.

ORANGE CREMA

We use this to top our tacos, burritos, and bowls made with Blackened Salmon (page 112), but it would go well with chicken or shrimp dishes, too. While we typically use fresh juices at the restaurant, orange juice concentrate delivers a lot of flavor without watering down the crema. Mayonnaise adds more acidity to balance out the sweetness of the orange.

Makes about 1 cup

½ cup sour cream

½ cup mayonnaise

½ cup orange juice concentrate, thawed

In a medium bowl, combine the sour cream, mayonnaise, and orange juice concentrate and mix well to combine. Use immediately or refrigerate in an airtight container for up to 3 days.

AVOCADO CREMA

CHEESY BEAN DIP

You can use this super simple bean dip in our Breakfast Burrito (page 132) or our BCR Burritos (page 139), add it to a quesadilla (pages 145–47), or serve it as intended, with tortilla chips and alongside some good salsa. It's also great served with scrambled eggs and hot sauce.

Makes about 2 cups

1 (16-ounce) can refried beans

½ cup cream cheese, at room temperature

1 cup shredded Mexican-style cheese blend, store-bought or homemade (see page 86)

1 tablespoon chopped pickled jalapeños

1 tablespoon pickled jalapeño juice

1 tablespoon crumbled Cotija

Hot sauce, such as Trejo's, Cholula, or Tapatío (optional)

Add the beans to a medium saucepan set over medium heat and stir occasionally until they are warmed through, about 5 minutes.

Add the cream cheese a spoonful at a time and stir to combine. Once combined, reduce the heat to low. Add the cheese blend and stir until thoroughly combined and melted. Add the pickled jalapeños and jalapeño juice. Serve hot, garnished with the Cotija and hot sauce, if desired.

CHIPOTLE SHRIMP COCKTAIL SAUCE

Let's face it: shrimp cocktail is really all about the sauce. You might notice that chipotle chiles in adobo sauce show up in a lot of our recipes. That's because they're so damn delicious, adding an incredible smoky-hot flavor to everything you mix them with—even sauce for a shrimp cocktail. I had the chefs put this sauce with shrimp on the menu because I love a steakhouse shrimp cocktail, but nobody ordered it (I guess it was too out there for a Mexican joint)—the sauce is so good, though, I wanted it to have a space in this book. You can serve it with some precooked shrimp from the grocery or poach your own, but I highly recommend serving it alongside the Citrus, Herb & Garlic Shrimp (page 102), which can be prepared in big batches, making it a perfect finger or fork-friendly party food. Your guests will thank you and you will thank me. You're welcome.

Makes about 1½ cups

4 chipotle chiles from a can of chipotle chiles in adobo sauce

Juice of 1 lime

1 tablespoon white balsamic vinegar

1 tablespoon molasses

2 tablespoons dark brown sugar

2 tablespoons soy sauce

1 cup ketchup

2 tablespoons bottled horseradish

Juice of ½ lemon

1 teaspoon Worcestershire sauce

Citrus, Herb & Garlic Shrimp (page 102) or poached shrimp

Finely chop the chipotles, mashing them against the cutting board until they form a smooth paste. Transfer the paste to a small saucepan, add the lime juice and vinegar, and whisk to combine. Stir in the molasses and sugar, and slowly warm the sauce over medium heat, stirring occasionally, until the sugar dissolves and the volume reduces to a paste consistency, about 3 minutes. Stir in the soy sauce and set it aside to cool.

In a medium bowl, combine the ketchup with the horseradish, lemon juice, and Worcestershire sauce. Stir in the cooled chipotle-molasses mixture. Cover the bowl with plastic wrap and refrigerate until chilled, about 30 minutes. Serve with the cooked shrimp. (The sauce can be refrigerated for up to 5 days.)

Angeleno Artistry

L.A. is my hometown, but Pacoima is my 'hood, and as a kid running around the neighborhood, I *was* a hood! Pacoima is in the San Fernando Valley, just west of the Angeles National Forest. One of the oldest parts of the city, it was a Native American settlement 1,500 years ago and a Spanish mission 200 years ago. Now, it's a town of 75,000 people. Like a lot of things in life, Pacoima is what you make of it. Like its other famous residents, including Chicano rock pioneer Ritchie Valens, two-time world boxing champion Bobby Chacon, and California Secretary of State Alex Padilla, I was lucky to make a lot out of it.

When I was a kid, Pacoima was known as one of the few places where, if you were a minority, you could buy a house. Which made it one of the most diverse parts of the city. That's true to this day: Latinos, African Americans, Japanese, Chinese, Caucasians, Catholics, Jews—we're all living together. Both the vice-principal at my school and my history teacher, Mrs. Findely, always told me I had potential and they taught me that what goes around comes around. Little did I know that I'd work my way out of Pacoima only to end up back there. I bought the house I grew up in and another around the corner where I keep my cars and recharge when I'm not on the road. I love it—this is home. Where else in the world can I drive down the street in one of my low-riders, look up, and see a mural of myself on the side of a building that isn't one of my restaurants? That's the beauty of Pacoima and the beauty of L.A. It's a living, breathing work of art.

People ask me what it was like growing up a Latino in L.A. in the 1950s and '60s. I got to tell you something—I never really experienced racism. People that I ran with, my gang, we were all people who had been thrown out of every other gang because of our general insanity—and we were a diverse crew. Frank Russo, an Italian, was one of the guys who saved my life, as far as getting clean and getting sober goes. Marty Hart was a white guy; Harry Ross was Jewish. We came from different backgrounds and we stood up for each other. No one ever told us we weren't allowed to go somewhere or be someplace.

Pacoima was hit hard by the housing crisis in 2008 and hundreds of houses in the neighborhood went into foreclosure. After the recession, a group of artists wanted to express civic pride and started painting murals throughout the city and on a stretch of Van Nuys Boulevard between Foothill Boulevard and San Fernando Road that's now called "Mural Mile." Among them there's one of Ritchie Valens, one of the Mona Lisa in a sombrero and bandolier like a badass *bandita*, one of the Virgin Mary with cyberpunk and Aztec symbols, and then there's one of me, shirtless, with a Chevy pickup and a motorcycle. When they unveiled the mural of me, there was a ceremony and I brought my mom; she couldn't help but remind me that I'd been arrested for selling drugs at the taco stand right across the way. I'm grateful that it's something I can laugh about today—and believe me, the irony of it all is not lost on me! I've never really left Pacoima to live anywhere else. Only when I have to be on set to film—but even then, I can't wait to get back home.

Tacos, Burritos, Bowls & Quesadillas

L.A.

has a long tradition of doing whatever the hell it wants with tacos and burritos. Back in the 1970s, a Hollywood restaurant called Oki-Dog started putting pastrami in burritos and the punk rockers loved them. Ten years ago a Korean-American dude named Roy Choi started selling Korean tacos loaded with kimchi and bulgogi out of a truck and made it a thing all over the world. At Trejo's we put falafel and chicken tikka in tacos, because why not, right? McDonald's even sells grilled chicken rolled up in a tortilla but they call it a "wrap." You can call it a wrap but it's still a damn burrito to me!

I really think my mom was the first taco artist. Sixty years ago she put a hot dog in a tortilla and handed it to me. The first time someone handed me a hot dog on a bun didn't happen until I was seven years old. I took one look at the bun and was like, "What the hell is this? This isn't a tortilla."

But really, is there anything more beautiful, more Los Angeles, than a taco? They're portable and affordable, and each region of Mexico is represented by the filling: fish tacos from Baja, *al pastor* from Mexico City, *birria* from Jalisco. When I was growing up, there were taco shops stuffing all the cuts that gringos wouldn't touch, like tongue and tripe, into a tortilla. Now you've got $1.50 tacos sold out of converted shopping carts with griddles made of cookie sheets, taco trucks, old-school taco stands, and restaurants selling fancy $14 tacos (yes, 14 bucks for *one* taco). L.A. is a taco metropolis if you keep your eyes peeled. Whether you're cruising down Cesar Chavez Avenue at night with your homies or hanging out with the fans near USC after a football game, you'll see the trucks, or little pop-up restaurants with utility lights clamped to tents, on corners with people gathered around representing every facet of Los Angeles: sports fans, punk rockers, delivery guys, neighborhood families with kids, and every generation from grandma to baby all eating tacos.

RESTAURANT TACOS *versus* HOME TACOS

The recipes in this chapter outline how we build our tacos, burritos, bowls, and quesadillas at the restaurant. If you've got time to make every single component, you're a champ. If you've been cooking sauces and salsas and dishes from this book and have a few components on hand, then you're halfway to a lot of these dishes already. If you want to try one of these for the first time and don't feel like including one component, like the *salsa verde* in the slaw for the Jackfruit Tacos (page 124), that's fine. (And, yes, real men eat jackfruit. I love it!) You don't need to utilize every single layer of flavor the way we do. It'll be darned good with just *pico de gallo*. There are no rules with tacos. Like we do in L.A., you can do whatever the hell you want with a taco.

The garnishes and sauces suggested in the recipes will only make them better, but you can also prepare a simple and delicious carnitas taco with just some chopped cilantro and onion, no salsa required.

BUILD A BETTER TACO

We are meticulous about taco toppings. Sure, you could just throw some meat on a tortilla and sling salsa and cilantro on top and call it done. But if you've ever been to one of our restaurants, you've seen that every taco is topped with care: the meat and beans and some of the toppings are in a straight line, evenly dispersed from one side of the tortilla to the other; some get a garnish of pickled onions, some get crema, some get a slaw. There's a logic to the visuals and in the eating experience. We eat with our eyes first, they say, so we make sure our tacos look as beautiful as possible when they hit the table. But looks only get you so far, and we fill the tacos just so, so that you have just enough of the different components to create harmony and excitement with each and every bite.

The FILLINGS

At my restaurants tacos are not junk food, unless you want them to be. We want everyone to be able to be satisfied: carnivores and vegetarians, pescatarians (people who eat fish but not meat) and vegans, flexitarians (that means a person who is mostly vegetarian but on occasion will eat a cow), gluten-free, and the undecided. So we make sure to have a variety of fillings, from the classic *carnitas* I grew up eating at *taquerias* and a version of the brisket inspired by Mom's recipe. But we have mushroom asada and jackfruit for the vegans, too.

Choose YOUR FORMAT

At Trejo's we're not unlike other Mexican joints in that you can pick your protein or other filling and have it in a taco or a burrito. We also offer low-carb bowls that basically are like supercharged salads.

Barbacoa Brisket

This brisket was inspired by Mom's recipe for *barbacoa*, the slow-cooked, tender, and flavorful Mexican version of brisket. While I'm never going to love anyone else's barbacoa more than hers, the Trejo's kitchen team works their magic with this one. They brine the meat in salt and sugar and aromatic spices for two whole freaking days. Brining seasons and tenderizes the meat so that when you finally cook it, it's unbelievably soft, tender, and full of sweet and spicy flavors. This is a project that will feed a family of four for several days, as tacos, burritos, or carved into slices and served with mashed potatoes (page 168) or rice (pages 171–72). The battle plan is to start brining the meat on Friday morning and start cooking it Sunday morning. After the brining is done, it's slow and low roasting all day, filling the house with wonderful aromas. Then you take the brisket out of the pan and reduce the braising juices until they make a rich and flavorful sauce. You will be eating very happily that evening . . . and for the rest of the week.

It also freezes well: Put your leftovers in a big resealable plastic freezer bag and keep it in the freezer until you're hungry again.

Serves 6

For Dry Brining

½ cup sugar

½ cup kosher salt

4 garlic cloves, finely chopped

2 tablespoons freshly ground black pepper (see Trejo's Tip, page 76)

2 teaspoons ground cumin

4 to 5 pounds beef brisket

For Browning and Braising

2 tablespoons vegetable oil

1 medium yellow onion, thinly sliced

1 garlic clove, roughly chopped

1 tablespoon chili powder

2 teaspoons ground coriander

2 teaspoons ground cumin

¼ cup apple cider vinegar

1 14½-ounce can whole peeled tomatoes, with their juices

2 chipotle chiles from a can of chipotle chiles in adobo sauce, chopped

2 dried bay leaves

¼ cup molasses

recipe continues

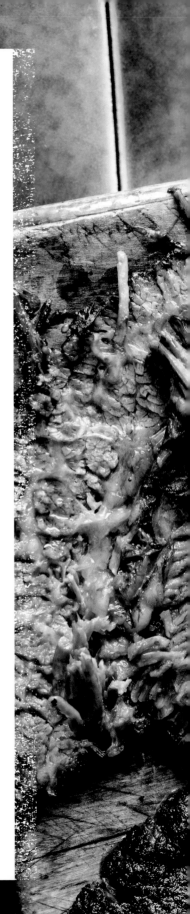

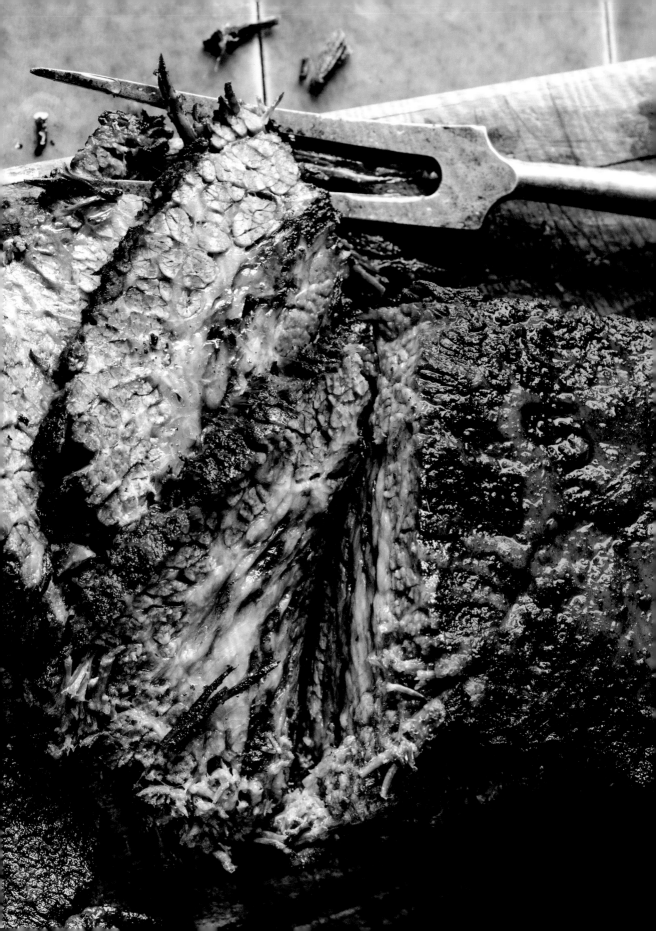

DRY-BRINE THE BRISKET   In a small bowl, combine the sugar, salt, garlic, pepper, and cumin and mix well.

Season the beef on both sides with the spice mixture. Wrap the beef in plastic wrap and place it in a large bowl or pan. Refrigerate for 48 hours.

BROWN AND BRAISE THE BRISKET   Preheat the oven to 325°F.

Place the brisket on your work surface, unwrap it, and wipe off the excess brining mixture. Heat a large heavy skillet (cast iron works well) over medium-high heat for 3 minutes. Then add the oil and heat just until it begins to smoke, about 2 minutes. Add the meat to the hot skillet and cook until it is browned on one side, 5 to 7 minutes, checking at 4 minutes to catch the brisket before the sugar in the rub begins to burn. Turn the brisket over and brown the other side for 5 to 7 minutes, checking at 4 minutes to prevent burning.

Transfer the meat to a deep roasting pan or Dutch oven, leaving the skillet on medium-high heat. Set the roasting pan aside.

Add the onion, garlic, chili powder, coriander, and cumin to the drippings in the skillet and stir until they are fragrant, about 30 seconds. Add the vinegar and boil until it's almost evaporated, scraping the skillet with a wooden spoon to get all the bits off the bottom. Crush the whole tomatoes through your fingers, letting them fall into the skillet. Add the tomato juice from the can and the chipotles, bay leaves, and molasses. Stir in 2 cups of water and pour the mixture over the brisket. Wrap the roasting pan tightly with aluminum foil to form a tight seal. Put the pan in the oven and cook until the brisket is fork-tender, about 5 hours.

FOR TACOS/BURRITOS/BOWLS   Transfer the brisket from the roasting pan to a bowl. Set the roasting pan over medium heat and cook the juices in the pan until they are reduced by half, about 10 minutes. Pour the sauce over the brisket and use two forks to pull it apart and shred the meat. Then make the tacos, burritos, or bowls as instructed in the recipes on pages 77 and 78.

FOR CARVED BRISKET   If you are going to carve the brisket to serve it as an entrée, transfer it to a cutting board. Set the roasting pan over medium heat and cook the juices in the pan until they are reduced by half, about 10 minutes. Pour the sauce into a small bowl or gravy dish. Using a very sharp knife, cut the brisket crosswise and against the grain into ¾-inch-thick slices. Serve with the sauce on the side.

Trejo's Tip

CRUSHING PEPPER

When you need a large amount of ground black pepper, rather than using a pepper grinder, you can quickly pulverize the pepper in a spice grinder if you have one; a mortar and pestle (like a molcajete) works great, too.

BARBACOA BRISKET TACOS

Braised *barbacoa* is so tender and soft, it benefits from the added crunch of fried tortilla strips.

Makes 12 tacos

12 6-inch corn tortillas
3 cups shredded Barbacoa Brisket (page 74)
1½ cups Pico de Gallo (page 48)
2 tablespoons crumbled Cotija cheese
½ cup fried tortilla strips (recipe follows)
2 limes, each cut into 6 wedges

Preheat the oven to 250°F.

Stack the tortillas, wrap them in aluminum foil, place them in the oven, and let them warm until they're fragrant and pliable, about 15 minutes.

Remove the tortillas from the oven. Unwrap the stack and line up the tortillas, assembly-line-style, on your work surface.

Spoon about ¼ cup of the brisket in a straight line down the center of each tortilla. Spoon a line of Pico de Gallo to the right of the brisket. Sprinkle the Cotija over the brisket and the pico, and sprinkle with the tortilla strips. Serve each taco with a lime wedge on the side.

HOMEMADE TORTILLA STRIPS (OR CHIPS)

It's easy to make tortilla strips and chips—just cut up tortillas and fry them (it's a great way to use up leftover tortillas). We scatter these on a bunch of our tacos and other dishes, but feel free to use them just the way you would croutons, sprinkling them on soups or salads, or just eat them straight out of the bowl.

Makes about 2 cups

2 cups neutral oil, such as canola or vegetable
6 6-inch corn tortillas, cut into strips approximately 2 inches long and ⅛ inch wide
Kosher salt, to taste

In a medium saucepan set over medium heat, heat the oil until it reaches 350°F.

Working in batches, and taking care not to crowd the pan, cook the tortilla strips, turning with a slotted spoon, until they're golden brown, 45 seconds to 1 minute. Remove the strips with the slotted spoon. Drain on a paper towel–lined plate. Season with salt. Store in an airtight container for up to 2 days.

BARBACOA BRISKET BURRITOS

Makes 4 burritos

4 13-inch flour tortillas
1 cup Basic Black Beans (page 170), warmed
2 cups shredded Barbacoa Brisket (page 74)
1 cup Pico de Gallo (page 48), drained
½ small red onion, finely chopped
¼ cup chopped fresh cilantro

Place a tortilla in a large skillet set over medium heat, warming it until it is heated through and lightly browned in spots, about 1 minute. Turn the tortilla over and warm it on the second side, 1 minute more. Transfer the tortilla to a plate and cover it with a kitchen towel to keep it warm. Repeat with the remaining tortillas.

Lay the tortillas out on your work surface. Spoon ¼ cup of the beans in a straight line across the middle of each tortilla. Place ½ cup of the brisket in a line on top of the beans. Line the Pico de Gallo to the right of the beans. Sprinkle the onion and cilantro over the top. Fold the left and right sides of each tortilla in by 1 inch. Grab the bottom of the tortilla and roll it away from you, ensuring that the sides are tucked in.

BARBACOA BRISKET BOWLS

Makes 4 bowls

2 cups Spanish Rice (page 171), warmed
2 cups Basic Black Beans (page 170), warmed
2 cups grilled corn (see page 163)
1 cup Pico de Gallo (page 48)
1 cup shredded romaine lettuce
2 cups shredded Barbacoa Brisket (page 74)
½ small red onion, finely chopped
¼ cup chopped fresh cilantro
¼ cup fried tortilla strips (see page 77)
¼ cup crumbled Cotija cheese
1 lime, cut into 4 wedges

In each individual serving bowl, arrange evenly divided portions of the rice, beans, corn, Pico de Gallo, lettuce, and brisket in a clockwise pattern. Garnish with the onion, cilantro, tortilla strips, and Cotija. Serve each bowl with a lime wedge on the side.

Carne Asada

Carne asada is one of my all-time-favorite dishes: it's easy to make, it uses affordable cuts of meat, and it's delicious. It's typically made with somewhat tough but full-flavored cuts like flank, flap, and skirt steak. The trick is to slice them thinly across the grain after cooking them on high heat. All that connective tissue that was tough will have melted over the heat, and cutting across the grain makes the fibers of the meat separate when you bite into them.

While soy sauce isn't a traditional Mexican ingredient, it's the secret to the success of our carne asada, adding deep flavor and seasoning the steak more than salt alone would. It's best to make this marinade a day in advance so you have time to let the flank steak marinate overnight before grilling it.

Serves 8

Marinade

- ½ large white onion, roughly chopped
- 3 chipotle chiles from a can of chipotle chiles in adobo sauce, plus 2 tablespoons of the sauce
- 2 medium jalapeños, roughly chopped
- 6 garlic cloves
- ½ cup roughly chopped fresh cilantro
- ¾ cup orange juice (preferably fresh)
- ½ cup pure olive oil
- ¼ cup soy sauce
- Juice of 1 lemon
- 1 tablespoon ground cumin
- 1 tablespoon smoked paprika
- 3 pounds flank, flap, or skirt steak

MARINATE THE STEAK Combine the onion, chipotles and sauce, jalapeños, garlic, cilantro, orange juice, olive oil, soy sauce, lemon juice, cumin, and paprika in a food processor or blender and puree. (See sidebar, page 83.) Transfer the marinade to a large self-seal plastic bag or airtight container.

Add the flank steak and turn to coat it in the marinade, then seal the bag (or cover the container). Refrigerate overnight.

GRILL THE STEAK Remove the steak from the marinade, letting the excess marinade drip back into the bag or bowl. Place the steak on a platter and set it aside at room temperature for 30 minutes.

Meanwhile, heat a gas or charcoal grill to medium-high heat.

Grill the steak until it is charred, about 5 minutes. Turn it over and grill until charred on the other side, about 5 minutes more. Transfer it to a cutting board and let it rest for 5 minutes before slicing it crosswise and against the grain.

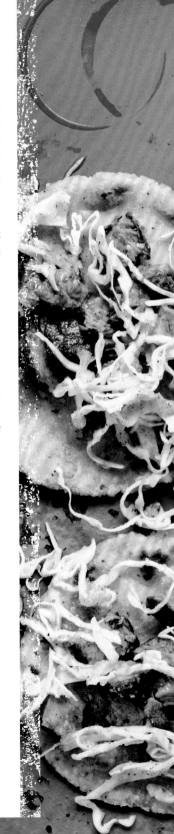

CARNE ASADA TACOS

Makes 12 tacos

12 6-inch tortillas
1½ cups shredded green cabbage
¼ cup Salsa Verde (page 52)
3 cups Carne Asada (page 80)
2 limes, each cut into 6 wedges

Preheat the oven to 250°F.

Stack the tortillas, wrap them in aluminum foil, place them in the oven, and let them warm until they're fragrant and pliable, about 15 minutes.

Remove the tortillas from the oven. Unwrap the stack and line up the tortillas, assembly-line-style, on your work surface.

In a medium bowl, mix the shredded cabbage with the Salsa Verde. Divide the Carne Asada among the tortillas, placing it in a straight line down the center of each tortilla. Place a line of the cabbage mixture to the right of the steak. Serve a lime wedge with each taco.

CARNE ASADA BOWLS

Makes 4 bowls

2 cups Spanish Rice (page 171), warmed

2 cups Basic Black Beans (page 170), warmed

2 cups grilled corn (see page 163)

1 cup Pico de Gallo (page 48)

1 cup shredded romaine lettuce

2 cups diced Carne Asada (page 80)

½ cup Pepita Pesto (page 56)

¼ cup finely chopped fresh cilantro

In each individual serving bowl, arrange evenly divided portions of the rice, beans, corn, Pico de Gallo, lettuce, and Carne Asada in a clockwise pattern. Top with the pesto and garnish with the cilantro.

TO BLEND OR NOT TO BLEND?

If you don't have a blender or food processor to make the carne asada marinade, that's fine. Our marinades are about the flavor, not the smoothness of the puree. Hand-chopping and -mixing ingredients might take a little more time, but a rough-cut marinade will still do the trick. Just be sure to scrape any extra bits of marinade off the meat before grilling so they don't get burned when you cook it.

CARNE ASADA BURRITOS

Makes 4 burritos

½ cup shredded cabbage

1 tablespoon Salsa Verde (page 52)

4 13-inch flour tortillas

½ cup shredded Mexican-style cheese blend, store-bought or homemade (see page 86)

1 cup Basic Black Beans (page 170), warmed

1 cup Spanish Rice (page 171), warmed

2 cups Carne Asada (page 80)

½ cup Pepita Pesto (page 56)

½ cup Salsa Roja (page 53)

In a medium bowl, combine the cabbage with the Salsa Verde and toss to coat the cabbage well.

Place a tortilla in a large skillet set over medium heat, warming it until it is heated through and lightly browned in spots, about 1 minute. Turn the tortilla over and warm on the second side, 1 minute more. Transfer the tortilla to a plate and cover it with a kitchen towel to keep it warm. Repeat with the remaining tortillas.

Lay the tortillas out on your work surface. Spoon 2 tablespoons of the cheese in a straight line across the middle of each tortilla. Layer ¼ cup of the beans, ¼ cup of the rice, ½ cup of the Carne Asada, and a quarter of the cabbage mixture over the cheese. Top with the Pepita Pesto. Fold the left and right sides of each tortilla in by 1 inch. Grab the bottom of the tortilla and roll it away from you, ensuring the sides are tucked in. Serve with the Salsa Roja on the side.

Carnitas

Carnitas means "little meats" in Spanish. Which doesn't seem to make a whole lot of sense when you're starting with a 5-pound hunk of pork that is by no means a "little meat." This is how it got its name: the pork shoulder is braised low and slow into submission with herbs and chiles. It becomes so tender that you can literally cut it with a spoon. After that, you take the pork and add it to a hot pan. As you press down on it to get it to crisp and brown, the pork shreds and makes those little pieces of incredibly flavorful meat.

Makes enough carnitas to fill about 20 tacos, or 10 burritos, or 10 bowls

2 tablespoons pure olive oil

5 pounds boneless pork shoulder, cut into 2-inch cubes

1 12-ounce package sliced bacon, cut crosswise into 2-inch pieces

1 tablespoon freshly ground black pepper

2 teaspoons ground cumin

2 teaspoons chopped dried chile de árbol or dried red pepper flakes

1 teaspoon dried oregano

2 teaspoons kosher salt

1 dried bay leaf

Preheat the oven to 350°F.

Set a large heavy-bottomed pot or Dutch oven over medium-high heat, add the oil, and heat until the oil is shimmering, about 2 minutes. Add the pork shoulder and the bacon. Cook until the pork is browned on both sides and the bacon is starting to render its fat, about 10 minutes.

Add the pepper, cumin, chile, oregano, salt, and bay leaf, and then pour in 4 cups of water (the water should come about halfway up the pork; add more if necessary). Bring the water to a boil and then place the pot, uncovered, in the oven. Cook the pork, turning it every 30 minutes, until it is tender and shreds easily, about 2 hours.

Remove the pot from the oven and use a slotted spoon to transfer the pork to a cutting board. Discard the bacon. Let the pork cool slightly, and then roughly chop it.

Heat a large cast-iron or nonstick skillet over medium-high heat for 2 minutes. Working in batches, place some of the pork in the pan (don't overcrowd the pan) and press down on it with a spatula until it is browned and crisp, about 5 minutes. Transfer the browned pork to a large bowl and repeat with the remaining pork. Serve the carnitas in tacos, burritos, or bowls.

GRILLED PINEAPPLE

There's just something about the pairing of salty, rich pork and sweet, tangy pineapple that makes it one of the most delicious combinations in the Mexican kitchen. Grilling pineapple to make a few tacos makes a lot of sense, because nobody ever complained about having leftover grilled pineapple. Just one request: Please don't use the canned fruit in these recipes! It can't hold a candle to grilled fresh pineapple — you're better off doing without.

Here's how to do it: With a big kitchen knife, cut the top off the pineapple; then cut the bottom off to make a stable base. Stand the pineapple upright and slice down the sides to remove the thick spiny skin, following the shape of the pineapple. Lay the pineapple down and slice it crosswise. Use a small round cookie cutter or biscuit cutter to punch out the core in each slice. Heat a gas or charcoal grill or grill pan to medium heat. Grill slices over medium heat until they are caramelized on both sides, about 3 minutes a side.

Use any leftovers on yogurt for breakfast, on ice cream, in salads, or as a snack on its own.

Trejo's Tip

GET CHEESY

At the restaurant we shred our own blend of mozzarella, Monterey Jack, and asadero cheese to fill our tacos, burritos, and quesadillas, but you can use any shredded Mexican-style cheese blend from the supermarket. The mixtures can vary a little and sometimes contain cheddar or queso quesadilla, but they all will work just fine.

CARNITAS TACOS

Makes 12 tacos

12 6-inch corn tortillas

3 cups Carnitas (page 84)

½ cup chopped grilled pineapple (optional; see sidebar)

½ cup Pickled Red Onions (page 50)

½ medium white onion, finely chopped

½ cup finely chopped fresh cilantro

1 lime, cut into 6 wedges

Hot sauce, such as Trejo's, Tapatío, or Cholula

Preheat the oven to 250°F.

Stack the tortillas, wrap them in aluminum foil, place them in the oven, and let them warm until they're fragrant and pliable, about 15 minutes.

Remove the tortillas from the oven. Unwrap the stack and line up the tortillas, assembly-line-style, on your work surface. Place a line of carnitas (about ¼ cup per taco) down the center of each tortilla. Top the carnitas with the grilled pineapple, if using, pickled onions, white onion, and cilantro. Serve with the lime wedges and hot sauce on the side.

CARNITAS BURRITOS

4 13-inch flour tortillas

1 cup Basic Black Beans (page 170), warmed

2 cups Carnitas (page 84), warmed

1 cup Spanish Rice (page 171), warmed

½ cup shredded Mexican-style cheese blend, store-bought or homemade (see Trejo's Tip, opposite)

Hot sauce, such as Trejo's, Tapatío, or Cholula

1 cup shredded red cabbage

1 cup Pico de Gallo (page 48), drained

½ cup chopped grilled pineapple (see sidebar, opposite)

¼ cup finely chopped red onion

¼ cup chopped fresh cilantro

¼ cup Salsa Roja (page 53)

Place a tortilla in a large skillet set over medium heat, warming it until it is heated through and lightly browned in spots, about 1 minute. Turn the tortilla over and warm it on the second side, 1 minute more. Transfer the tortilla to a plate and cover it with a kitchen towel to keep it warm. Repeat with the remaining tortillas.

Lay the tortillas out on your work surface. Add ¼ cup of the beans in a straight line across the middle of each tortilla. Layer ½ cup of the carnitas and ¼ cup of the rice on top of the beans. Add the cheese. Drizzle with hot sauce to taste. Add the cabbage and Pico de Gallo. Sprinkle the pineapple, onion, and cilantro over the fillings. Fold the left and right sides of each tortilla in by 1 inch. Grab the bottom of the tortilla and roll it away from you, ensuring the sides are tucked in. Serve with the Salsa Roja on the side.

CARNITAS BOWLS

2 cups Spanish Rice (page 171), warmed

2 cups Basic Black Beans (page 170), warmed

2 cups grilled corn (see page 163)

1 cup Pico de Gallo (page 48)

1 cup shredded romaine lettuce

2 cups Carnitas (page 84)

½ cup hot sauce, such as Trejo's, Cholula, or Tapatío

¼ cup chopped grilled pineapple (see sidebar, opposite)

¼ cup finely chopped red onion

¼ cup chopped fresh cilantro

In each individual serving bowl, arrange evenly divided portions of the rice, beans, corn, Pico de Gallo, lettuce, and carnitas in a clockwise pattern. Drizzle with the hot sauce and serve sprinkled with the pineapple, onion, and cilantro.

Chicken Tikka

An Indian taco might not be the most common thing—not even in L.A., where people do all kinds of strange things to tacos. But when you try this, it'll make complete sense. It's actually not that far off from the tangy, orange-colored and cumin-spiked *al pastor* pork tacos you can find at taco trucks throughout the city. That is *if* you end up making tacos—the chicken tikka is so good, you may just end up eating it on its own!

Serves 4 to 6

Tikka Sauce

- 2 tablespoons canola oil
- 1 medium white or yellow onion, halved lengthwise and sliced crosswise
- 1 tablespoon brown or black mustard seeds
- 1½ teaspoons ground ginger
- 1½ teaspoons garlic powder
- 1 teaspoon asafetida (see Trejo's Tip, page 90)
- 2 tablespoons ground cumin
- 2 tablespoons coriander seeds
- 1 tablespoon ground turmeric
- ½ teaspoon cayenne pepper
- 1 cup canned peeled whole tomatoes, with their juice
- 1 tablespoon kosher salt
- ½ cup distilled white vinegar
- 1 cinnamon stick

Chicken Tikka

- 2 tablespoons canola oil
- 2 pounds boneless, skinless chicken breasts or thighs, cut into ½-inch pieces
- 1½ teaspoons kosher salt
- 1 teaspoon freshly ground black pepper

recipe continues

Trejo's Tips

SECRET INGREDIENT

Asafetida, an ingredient that's common in Indian cooking, gives dishes a uniquely garlicky and funky/pungent note. Used in small amounts and alongside other ingredients, it adds just one more layer of flavor. Like everything these days, it's easy to get on Amazon, though it might also be available at your local supermarket or Indian market or spice shop. If you don't have it, it's totally optional. The tikka will still be great — but it is kind of the magical ingredient that brings the dish from great to *wow*.

SAVING TIKKA SAUCE

This recipe makes 3 cups of sauce, so you can reserve half of it, freeze it in an airtight container, and use it later in the month.

MAKE THE TIKKA SAUCE   In a large saucepan set over medium-high heat, heat the canola oil until it is shimmering, about 2 minutes. Add the onion and sauté, stirring occasionally, until it is lightly browned, 5 to 7 minutes. Stir in the mustard seeds, ginger, garlic powder, asafetida, cumin, coriander seeds, turmeric, and cayenne and cook until the mixture is aromatic, about 1 minute. Add the tomatoes, salt, vinegar, cinnamon stick, and ½ cup of water, and bring everything to a boil. Reduce the heat to medium-low and simmer until the sauce has thickened slightly and the flavors have melded, about 10 minutes. Remove the cinnamon stick. Transfer the sauce to a blender and puree until completely smooth.

COOK THE CHICKEN   Place a large skillet over high heat until it is hot, about 2 minutes. Add the oil and heat until it is shimmering, about 1 minute. Add the chicken, season it with the salt and pepper, and cook, without stirring, until the chicken is browned on the bottom, about 5 minutes. Then stir and cook for 3 minutes more, until the chicken is lightly browned all over but not fully cooked through. Add 1½ cups of the tikka sauce (see Trejo's Tip) and stir to combine. Cook until the chicken is nicely glazed and cooked through, about 3 minutes. Serve in tacos, burritos, or bowls, or over rice.

CHICKEN TIKKA TACOS

Makes 8 tacos

8 5- to 6-inch flour tortillas

½ cup Escabeche-Mint Crema (page 58)

½ cup Spanish Rice (page 171), warmed

2 cups Chicken Tikka (page 88)

1 cup Pico de Gallo (page 48)

2 limes, quartered

Preheat the oven to 250°F.

Stack the tortillas, wrap them in aluminum foil, place them in the oven, and let them warm until they're fragrant and pliable, about 15 minutes.

Remove the tortillas from the oven. Unwrap the stack and line up the tortillas, assembly-line-style, on your work surface. Spoon the Escabeche-Mint Crema in a straight line down the middle of each tortilla, from edge to edge. Place the rice on top of the crema and then the chicken on top of the rice. Spoon the Pico de Gallo over the chicken. Serve with the lime wedges on the side.

CHICKEN TIKKA BURRITOS

Makes 4 burritos

4 13-inch flour tortillas

½ cup shredded Mexican-style cheese blend, store-bought or homemade (see page 86)

1 cup Spanish Rice (page 171), warmed

1 cup Basic Black Beans (page 170), warmed

2 cups Chicken Tikka (page 88)

1 cup Pico de Gallo (page 48), drained

½ cup Salsa Roja (page 53)

½ cup Escabeche-Mint Crema (page 58)

Place a tortilla in a large skillet set over medium heat, warming it until it is heated through and lightly browned in spots, about 1 minute. Turn the tortilla over and warm it on the second side, 1 minute more. Transfer the tortilla to a plate and cover it with a kitchen towel to keep it warm. Repeat with the remaining tortillas.

Lay the tortillas out on your work surface. Spoon 2 tablespoons of the cheese in a straight line across the middle of each tortilla. Layer ¼ cup of the rice, ¼ cup of the beans, and ½ cup of the chicken on top of the cheese. Add ¼ cup of the Pico de Gallo. Fold the left and right sides of each tortilla in by 1 inch. Grab the bottom of the tortilla and roll it away from you, ensuring the sides are tucked in. Serve with the Salsa Roja and Escabeche-Mint Crema on the side.

CHICKEN TIKKA BOWLS

Makes 4 bowls

2 cups Spanish Rice (page 171), warmed

2 cups Basic Black Beans (page 170), warmed

2 cups grilled corn (see page 163)

1 cup Pico de Gallo (page 48)

1 cup shredded romaine lettuce

2 cups Chicken Tikka (page 88)

½ cup Escabeche-Mint Crema (page 58)

¼ cup finely chopped fresh cilantro

In each individual serving bowl, arrange evenly divided portions of the rice, beans, corn, Pico de Gallo, lettuce, and chicken in a clockwise pattern. Top with the Escabeche-Mint Crema and garnish with the cilantro.

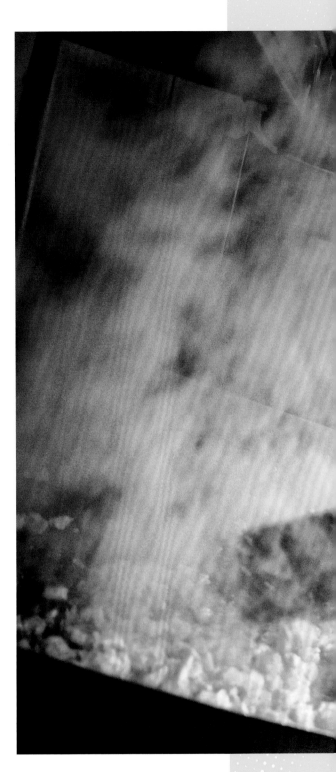

Trejo's Grilled Chicken

This is the chicken that we use to make our grilled chicken tacos, bowls, and burritos. Of course you can also cook the chicken and simply serve it with rice or on a salad. Salting the breast *before* adding the marinade is a little extra step we take to help ensure maximum flavor and tenderness.

Serves 4 to 6

Juice of 1 lime

1 tablespoon adobo sauce from a can of chipotle chiles

1 tablespoon sweet paprika

1 teaspoon ground cumin

1 teaspoon dried oregano

2 boneless, skinless chicken breasts or thighs, halved lengthwise to make 4 thin chicken cutlets

2 teaspoons kosher salt

1 teaspoon freshly ground black pepper

MARINATE THE CHICKEN In a large bowl, whisk together the lime juice, adobo sauce, paprika, cumin, and oregano.

Season the chicken with the salt and pepper, and then place the chicken in the marinade. Cover the bowl with plastic wrap and let the chicken marinate in the refrigerator for at least 1 hour or overnight.

GRILL THE CHICKEN Remove the chicken cutlets from the marinade, letting the excess drip back into the bowl. Place the chicken on a platter and let it sit at room temperature for 30 minutes (this is so the chicken will cook more quickly and evenly, making for juicier chicken).

Meanwhile, heat a gas or charcoal grill to medium-high heat. (For instructions on pan-searing, see sidebar, page 97.)

Add the chicken to the grill and cook until it is nicely charred, about 5 minutes. Turn the chicken over and cook until the other side has grill marks, about 5 minutes, and the chicken is cooked through. Remove the chicken from the grill. Chop into ½-inch cubes.

GRILLED CHICKEN TACOS

Makes 12 tacos

12 6-inch corn tortillas

1½ cups shredded cabbage

¼ cup Salsa Verde (page 52)

1 recipe Trejo's Grilled Chicken (page 94), chopped into small pieces

1 cup Pico de Gallo (page 48)

2 limes, each cut into 6 wedges

Preheat the oven to 250°F.

Stack the tortillas, wrap them in aluminum foil, place them in the oven, and let them warm until they're fragrant and pliable, about 15 minutes.

Remove the tortillas from the oven. Unwrap the stack and line up the tortillas, assembly-line-style, on your work surface.

In a medium bowl, mix the shredded cabbage with the Salsa Verde. Arrange the chicken in a straight line down the center of each tortilla. Place a line of the cabbage mixture on top of the chicken and a line of Pico de Gallo on top of the cabbage. Serve each taco with a lime wedge.

GRILLED CHICKEN BURRITOS

Makes 4 burritos

½ cup shredded cabbage

1 tablespoon Salsa Verde (page 52)

4 13-inch flour tortillas

½ cup shredded Mexican-style cheese blend, store-bought or homemade (see page 86)

1 cup Spanish Rice (page 171), warmed

1 cup Basic Black Beans (page 170), warmed

1 recipe Trejo's Grilled Chicken (page 94), diced (2 cups)

½ cup Pico de Gallo (page 48)

½ cup Salsa Roja (page 53)

In a medium bowl, combine the cabbage with the Salsa Verde, tossing to coat it well.

Place a tortilla in a large skillet set over medium heat, warming it until it is heated through and lightly browned in spots, about 1 minute. Turn the tortilla over and warm it on the second side, 1 minute more. Transfer the tortilla to a plate and cover it with a kitchen towel to keep it warm. Repeat with the remaining tortillas.

Lay the tortillas out on your work surface. Spoon 2 tablespoons of the cheese in a straight line across the middle of each tortilla. Layer ¼ cup of the rice, ¼ cup of the beans, and ½ cup of the chicken on top of the cheese. Add 2 tablespoons of the Pico de Gallo and 2 tablespoons of the cabbage mixture. Fold the left and right sides of each tortilla in by 1 inch. Grab the bottom of the tortilla and roll it away from you, ensuring the sides are tucked in. Serve with the Salsa Roja on the side.

GRILLED CHICKEN BOWLS

Makes 4 bowls

2 cups Spanish Rice (page 171), warmed

2 cups Basic Black Beans (page 170), warmed

2 cups grilled corn (see page 163)

1 cup Pico de Gallo (page 48)

1 cup shredded romaine lettuce

1 recipe Trejo's Grilled Chicken (page 94),
  diced (2 cups)

½ cup Salsa Verde (page 52)

¼ cup finely chopped fresh cilantro

In each individual bowl, arrange evenly divided portions of the rice, beans, corn, Pico de Gallo, lettuce, and chicken in a clockwise pattern. Top with the Salsa Verde and garnish with the cilantro.

PAN-SEARING AT HIGH HEAT

At Trejo's our griddles run 500°F, which allows us to char meat in a way few home cooks ever attempt. If you want to pan-sear your chicken or other protein rather than grill it, this is the time to turn on your overhead exhaust fan if you've got one and open the windows. Heat a large cast-iron pan or skillet over high heat for 2 minutes. Add 2 tablespoons neutral oil, like safflower or canola, and heat until it starts to smoke, 3 to 5 minutes. Then add your protein and cook as directed in the recipe you're using.

Trejo's Fried Chicken

I love our fried chicken. We add a bunch of spices, including cayenne for kick, and we fry it until it's super-crispy. This fried chicken is delicious on its own, but when you pair it with salsa and load it into tacos and burritos or even lettuce wraps, it's a whole other level of delicious. Taking the chicken out of the refrigerator 30 minutes before frying lets it come up to room temperature so it cooks quickly and more evenly. While it's warming up, you may as well give it a little extra attention by rubbing it down with salt as it sits—the salt is the equivalent of a light cure, which makes the meat even more flavorful and juicy.

Serves 4

- 1½ pounds boneless, skinless chicken thighs
- 3 teaspoons kosher salt
- 4 cups all-purpose flour
- 2 tablespoons garlic powder
- 2 tablespoons onion powder
- 1½ teaspoons dried oregano
- 1½ teaspoons sweet paprika
- ½ teaspoon cayenne pepper
- ½ teaspoon freshly ground black pepper
- 4 cups canola oil
- 2 cups buttermilk

Cut the chicken thighs into 1-inch-wide strips. Place the strips in a bowl and season them with 2 teaspoons of the salt. Set the chicken aside for 30 minutes at room temperature.

In a medium bowl, whisk together the flour, garlic powder, onion powder, oregano, paprika, cayenne, remaining teaspoon salt, and black pepper.

Heat the oil in a large heavy-bottomed pot set over medium-high heat until it reaches 350°F on an instant-read thermometer.

recipe continues

Drain off any liquid in the bowl of chicken and pour the buttermilk over the chicken. Lift the chicken pieces out of the buttermilk, letting the excess drip back into the bowl, and then dredge them through the spiced flour, shaking off any excess. Slowly lower a few chicken pieces (you don't want to overcrowd the pot) into the hot oil and cook, turning them often, until they are golden brown, 7 to 10 minutes. To check if it's done, remove a piece of chicken and test its internal temperature with an instant-read thermometer—it should read 165°F. Drain the fried chicken on a wire rack or paper towels, and repeat with the remaining pieces. Serve hot or at room temperature.

FRIED CHICKEN TACOS

Instead of corn tortillas, you can have this in a lettuce wrap, which makes it, in California In-N-Out terminology, "protein style," so you could say it's sort of half healthy.

Makes 12 tacos

12 6-inch corn tortillas or leaves of Bibb lettuce
2 cups shredded red cabbage
½ cup Chipotle Crema (page 60)
2 tablespoons pure olive oil
Kosher salt, to taste
Freshly ground black pepper, to taste
1 recipe Trejo's Fried Chicken (page 98)
1½ cups Pico de Gallo (page 48)

Preheat the oven to 250°F.

Stack the tortillas, wrap them in aluminum foil, place them in the oven, and let them warm until they're fragrant and pliable, about 15 minutes.

Meanwhile, in a medium bowl, combine the cabbage, ¼ cup of the Chipotle Crema, and olive oil and season with a little salt and pepper if needed. Set aside.

Remove the tortillas from the oven. Unwrap the stack and line up the tortillas, assembly-line-style, on your work surface. Divide the cabbage slaw among the tortillas, placing it in a line down the center. Top with the fried chicken, drizzle the chicken with the remaining Chipotle Crema, and serve topped with the Pico de Gallo.

FRIED CHICKEN BURRITOS

Makes 4 burritos

1 cup shredded red cabbage
¼ cup Chipotle Crema (page 60)
1 tablespoon pure olive oil
Kosher salt, to taste
Freshly ground black pepper, to taste
4 13-inch flour tortillas
½ cup shredded Mexican-style cheese blend, store-bought or homemade (see page 86)
1 cup Spanish Rice (page 171), warmed
1 cup Basic Black Beans (page 170), warmed
1 recipe Trejo's Fried Chicken (page 98), chopped (2 cups)
1 cup Pico de Gallo (page 48), drained

In a medium bowl, combine the cabbage, 1 tablespoon of the Chipotle Crema, and the olive oil, and season with a little salt and pepper.

Place a tortilla in a large skillet set over medium heat, warming it until it is heated through and lightly browned in spots, about 1 minute. Turn the tortilla over and warm it on the second side, 1 minute more. Transfer the tortilla to a plate and cover it with a kitchen towel to keep it warm. Repeat with the remaining tortillas.

Lay the tortillas out on your work surface. Sprinkle 2 tablespoons of the cheese in a straight line across the middle of each tortilla. Layer ¼ cup of the rice, ¼ cup of the beans, and ½ cup of the fried chicken on top of the cheese. Top with ¼ cup of the slaw and ¼ cup of the Pico de Gallo. Fold the left and right sides of each tortilla in by 1 inch. Grab the bottom of the tortilla and roll it away from you, ensuring the sides are tucked in.

Citrus, Herb & Garlic Shrimp

This shrimp preparation is what goes on our Shrimp Tostadas (page 104), but since a tostada is really nothing more than an open-faced crunchy taco, you can serve it on tacos or in bowls or burritos, too. It also pairs well with our Chipotle Shrimp Cocktail Sauce (page 64). Use the shrimp instead of fish in the Classic Fish Tacos recipe on page 106 or instead of the shrimp in the Spicy Diablo Shrimp Burritos (page 120).

Serves 4 to 6

- 6 scallions, white and pale green parts, cut into 1-inch lengths
- ¼ cup roughly chopped fresh flat-leaf parsley
- ¼ cup roughly chopped fresh cilantro
- 1 tablespoon grated lemon zest (from 1 to 2 lemons)
- 1 tablespoon grated lime zest (from 3 to 4 limes)
- 2 garlic cloves, finely chopped
- 1 teaspoon kosher salt
- ½ cup pure olive oil
- 2 pounds medium shrimp, peeled, and deveined

Put the scallions, parsley, cilantro, citrus zest, garlic, and salt in a food processor or blender and pulse to finely chop. Transfer the mixture to a large bowl and stir in the olive oil. Add the shrimp and stir to coat well. Marinate the shrimp for at least 30 minutes or up to 1 hour.

Meanwhile, heat a gas or charcoal grill to medium-high heat.

Remove shrimp from marinade, letting excess marinade drip off. Grill the shrimp until they are no longer opaque and are lightly charred, about 3 minutes. Turn them over and grill the other side until cooked through, about 3 minutes more. Use the shrimp to make tostadas, tacos, burritos, and more.

Trejo's Tips

DIY TOSTADAS

Mexican markets and lots of groceries around L.A. sell crunchy prepared tostadas in the tortilla section. (Yes, we have vast tortilla sections at supermarkets in L.A. Yes, I love L.A.) If you can't find them at yours, just make your own: Fill a large deep saucepan with at least 2 inches of vegetable or other neutral oil. Heat it over medium-high heat until it reaches 350°F on an instant-read thermometer. Using tongs, gently fry 6-inch corn tortillas, one by one, until golden brown, about 1 minute. Drain the tostadas on paper towels or on a wire rack. Let them cool and they'll firm up and turn crunchy.

TRY TAJÍN

If you've ever had cut fruit from a street vendor in L.A., you have probably become acquainted with Tajín. It's the chile and lime–flavored red spice mix that every Mexican kid grew up eating, sprinkled on fruit and even on cucumber. It's one of those clever ways Mexican moms would get kids to eat their vegetables. Buy a bottle and use it on our Shrimp Tostadas and fish tacos, but don't hold back from using it in margarita salt or sprinkling it on cut mango or watermelon.

SHRIMP TOSTADAS

Makes 8 tostadas

2 small oranges

8 5-inch tostadas, store-bought or homemade (see Trejo's Tip)

2 avocados, halved, pitted, peeled, and thinly sliced

1½ cups shredded lettuce

1 pint cherry tomatoes, quartered

1 recipe Citrus, Herb & Garlic Shrimp (page 102)

Tajín seasoning (see Trejo's Tip)

½ cup finely chopped fresh cilantro

Cut the ends off of each orange. Stand the oranges upright and slice off the rind to expose the flesh, slicing from top to bottom and following the curve of the fruit. Slice between each segment to release the citrus and collect the pieces in a bowl.

Place the tostadas on your work surface and arrange the sliced avocado over the tostadas. Top the avocado with the lettuce. Arrange the orange segments, tomatoes, and shrimp over the lettuce. Season with Tajín to taste, garnish with the cilantro, and serve.

CLASSIC FISH TACOS

This taco is simple, with very few components that need cooking, and it makes a great 20-minute weeknight meal. It's the healthiest of the three fish tacos we serve because it's pan-cooked and not fried. If you're a pescatarian, you're going to love these. You could eat these every day and probably live forever.

Makes 8 tacos

1½ pounds fresh cod, cut into 3-inch pieces

Kosher salt

Freshly ground black pepper

4 tablespoons pure olive oil

1 lime, halved

1 cup shredded red or green cabbage

¼ cup Cumin Crema (page 60)

¼ cup chopped fresh cilantro

8 6-inch corn tortillas

¼ cup Pico de Gallo (page 48)

Pat the cod dry with paper towels and season it with salt and pepper. In a large pan set over medium-high heat, heat 2 tablespoons of the oil until it is just shimmering, about 2 minutes. Add the cod and cook until the pieces are lightly browned and just cooked through, about 3 minutes per side. Use a spatula to transfer the cooked cod to a large plate, and then squeeze the lime halves over it.

In a medium bowl, combine the cabbage with the remaining 2 tablespoons oil, the Cumin Crema, and the cilantro. Season with salt to taste.

Preheat the oven to 250°F.

Stack the tortillas, wrap them in aluminum foil, place them in the oven, and let them warm until they're fragrant and pliable, about 15 minutes.

Remove the tortillas from the oven. Unwrap the stack and line up the tortillas, assembly-line-style, on your work surface. Place a dollop of the slaw mixture on each tortilla. Top it with the fish and Pico de Gallo, and serve.

From Dusk to Dawn

in Trejo's Tacos

Throughout Los Angeles, from LAX to Pasadena, seven days a week, the cooks, bakers, bartenders, and bussers of Trejo's restaurants are cranking. Here's a snapshot of what goes on in an average day.

3:30 AM: The bakers show up at Trejo's Coffee & Donuts in Hollywood and begin to proof the 4 batches of dough that get made into the 1,000 donuts they sell daily.

5:00 AM: Counter staff and cooks arrive at the LAX location. They fry tater tots and roll up breakfast burritos before the morning rush—they'll blow through 100 burritos by noon.

6:00 AM: Local tortilla factory La Princesita drops off its daily delivery of fresh corn and flour tortillas.

6:30 AM: City Bean on La Brea drops off its freshly roasted custom blend of coffee beans at each location.

9:00 AM: Cooks at all the locations, from La Brea to Pasadena, start prepping for the day. They grill ears of corn, braise the jackfruit, chop and mix gallons of Pico de Gallo, Salsa Verde, and Salsa Roja, and sear off the carne asada. The team goes through 9,000 pounds of flap meat a month.

10:00 AM: A group of customers at the LAX location order breakfast burritos and a round of shots and beers.

11:00 AM: The commissary kitchen in Silver Lake bakes off 800 mini donuts for a wedding.

12:30 PM: Danny sings "Happy Birthday" to a group of women at Trejo's Cantina in Woodland Hills. He greets guests and fans, signs T-shirts and hats, and poses for selfies with everyone.

3:00 PM: After the lunch rush, the manager and bar manager of the Hollywood Cantina inventory the 100 tequilas and mezcals to see what needs to be reordered.

4:00 PM: The back of house sit down to a family meal of enchiladas while the floor staff review the manager's specials and what they're pushing that night.

5:30 PM: It's happy hour. A group of friends orders a round of margaritas and street tacos.

7:30 PM: The pre-theater dinner rush peaks in Pasadena as diners hurry to finish their meals before 8 o'clock curtain call.

9:30 PM: The final flight from Vegas lands at LAX and a group of passengers order the last burritos of the day.

11:00 PM: The valet folds up the red umbrella outside the La Brea location.

MIDNIGHT: The night crew at the La Brea location loads the Legos in the dishwasher so kids can play with clean ones the next day.

OG BEER-BATTERED FRIED FISH TACOS

Not all fish tacos are created equal: you've got your Baja Fish Tacos (page 110) that are battered and fried, you've got your basic healthy-ish pan-seared fish tacos (page 106), and then you've got the variations we've played with. We've had fried fish tacos on our menu from the beginning and have served two versions: one, the OG, is beer-battered; the Baja Fish Tacos are tortilla chip–battered. They're both incredible, so we're going to share both of them with you.

Makes 8 tacos

¾ cup all-purpose flour

¼ cup cornstarch

1½ teaspoons paprika

1 teaspoon kosher salt, plus extra to taste

¼ teaspoon baking powder

1 cup cold light Mexican beer, such as Modelo Especial

1 cup shredded red or green cabbage

1 cup Pico de Gallo (page 48)

¼ cup Lime Crema (page 59)

¼ cup finely chopped fresh cilantro

2 tablespoons pure olive oil

4 cups canola oil

1½ pounds fresh cod, cut into 2-inch pieces

8 6-inch flour or corn tortillas

In a medium bowl, combine the flour, cornstarch, paprika, salt, and baking powder and mix well. While lightly whisking, slowly pour in the beer. Do not overmix—you want the batter to be a little frothy. If you're not going to fry your fish immediately, keep the batter cool by placing the bowl in a larger bowl filled with ice.

In another medium bowl, combine the cabbage, Pico de Gallo, Lime Crema, cilantro, and olive oil and mix well. Season to taste with salt and set aside.

In a large deep pot set over medium-high heat, heat the canola oil until it reaches 350°F on an instant-read thermometer. Working in batches, coat the fish in the beer batter and gently lower it into the hot oil, taking care not to crowd the pot. Fry the fish, turning the pieces often, until they are golden brown, about 3 minutes. Transfer them to a wire rack to drain. Let the oil return to 350°F before frying the next batch of fish.

Preheat the oven to 250°F.

Stack the tortillas, wrap them in aluminum foil, place them in the oven, and let them warm until they're fragrant and pliable, about 15 minutes.

Remove the tortillas from the oven. Unwrap the stack and line up the tortillas, assembly-line-style, on your work surface. Place a few pieces of fish on each tortilla, and top them with the cabbage slaw.

BAJA FISH TACOS

Down in Baja, just south of the California–Mexico border, fried fish tacos are synonymous with street food in the coastal beach towns. We use tortillas every which way you (and we) can imagine. But would you ever think we'd pulverize fried tortilla chips in a blender until they're like flour and then coat fish in it and fry it? It adds this incredible additional crunch and flavor to our Baja Fish Tacos. (You can also use this preparation on shrimp.) These tacos are topped with sweet-hot mango salsa and tangy spicy Tajín.

Makes 8 tacos

1 12-ounce bag tortilla chips

2 cups rice flour

2 cups buttermilk

1½ pounds fresh cod, cut into 2-inch pieces

Oil for frying

8 6-inch flour or corn tortillas

2 cups shredded green cabbage

¼ cup Chipotle Crema (page 60)

1 cup Avocado Crema (page 61)

½ cup store-bought mango salsa

1 tablespoon Tajín seasoning (see Trejo's Tip, page 104)

BREAD AND FRY THE FISH   In a food processor, finely grind the tortilla chips until they form a fine powder. In three separate bowls, place the rice flour, buttermilk, and ground tortilla chips. One piece at a time, dredge the fish in the flour first, shaking off the excess. Then dunk it in the buttermilk, letting the excess drip back into the bowl. Lastly, dredge the fish through the ground tortilla chips, making sure to coat all sides. Set the fish aside on a plate or platter.

Fill a large deep pot halfway with oil. Heat over medium-high heat until the oil reaches 350°F on an instant-read thermometer. Working in batches, gently lower a few pieces of fish into the hot oil. Fry, turning the fish occasionally, until they are golden brown, about 3 minutes. Transfer the fish to a wire rack or to paper towels to drain. Let the oil come back up to 350°F before adding the next batch of fish.

MAKE THE TACOS   Preheat the oven to 250°F.

Stack the tortillas, wrap them in aluminum foil, place them in the oven, and let them warm until they're fragrant and pliable, about 15 minutes.

Remove the tortillas from the oven. Unwrap the stack and line up the tortillas, assembly-line-style, on your work surface.

In a medium mixing bowl, combine the cabbage with the Chipotle Crema. Spread a line of Avocado Crema down the center of each tortilla. Place 2 pieces of fish on the Avocado Crema and then add a spoonful of mango salsa in between the pieces of fish. Garnish with the cabbage mixture. Sprinkle with Tajín and serve.

Blackened Salmon

We call this "blackened salmon" because it's an homage to the old Cajun preparation in which a piece of fish is coated in so many spices, and so much pepper, that it looks black after a quick sear in a hot pan. The Cajuns used butter, which would char and burn a little. We like to do things a little healthier than that, so we skip the butter and push the chili powder. And while we do cook it over high heat, it doesn't get very black—just seared in spots.

Serves 4

- 3 tablespoons chili powder
- 2 teaspoons ground coriander
- 2 teaspoons freshly ground black pepper
- 1 teaspoon ground fennel
- 1 teaspoon dried thyme
- 1 teaspoon kosher salt
- 1 1½-pound salmon fillet, skin removed, cut into four 6-inch strips
- 2 tablespoons vegetable oil

In a medium bowl, mix the chili powder, coriander, pepper, fennel, thyme, and salt. Toss the salmon pieces in the spices to coat them thoroughly on all sides, shaking off any excess.

In a large skillet set over medium-high heat, heat the oil until it's just smoking, about 3 minutes. Place the salmon in the skillet and cook until it is browned on the bottom and cooked halfway through (it should no longer be translucent on the bottom half), about 2 minutes. Turn the salmon over and cook until it is firm and no longer translucent at all, about 2 minutes more.

Serve the cooked salmon in any of our fish taco preparations or in a bowl.

BLACKENED SALMON TACOS

Cherry tomatoes taste supersweet when you pair them with the spicy salmon. Orange Crema (page 61) cools everything down.

Makes 12 tacos

12 6-inch corn tortillas

1 tablespoon canola oil

1 cup cherry tomatoes, left whole

1 cup fresh corn kernels (from about 1 ear)

½ cup Orange Crema (page 61)

2 cups shredded green or red cabbage

Kosher salt

Freshly ground black pepper

1 recipe Blackened Salmon (page 112), cut into 1-inch pieces

2 limes, each cut into 6 wedges

Preheat the oven to 250°F.

Stack the tortillas, wrap them in aluminum foil, place them in the oven, and let them warm until they're fragrant and pliable, about 15 minutes.

Remove the tortillas from the oven. Unwrap the stack and line up the tortillas, assembly-line-style, on your work surface.

Heat the oil in a medium skillet set over medium heat until it is smoking, about 3 minutes. Add the cherry tomatoes and the corn, and cook until the tomatoes are slightly blistered and the corn is lightly toasted, about 2 minutes. Remove the skillet from the heat and set aside.

In a medium bowl, combine ¼ cup of the Orange Crema with the cabbage and mix well. Season with salt and pepper to taste.

Divide the remaining ¼ cup Orange Crema among the tortillas, spreading it over the center of each one. Add the salmon in a straight line down the center, top with the tomato/corn mixture, and garnish with the cabbage slaw. Serve each taco with a lime wedge.

BLACKENED SALMON BOWLS

Makes 4 bowls

2 cups Spanish Rice (page 171), warmed

2 cups Basic Black Beans (page 170), warmed

2 cups grilled corn (see page 163)

1 cup Pico de Gallo (page 48)

1 cup shredded romaine lettuce

1 recipe Blackened Salmon (page 112),
   cut into 1-inch pieces

¼ cup Orange Crema (page 61)

¼ cup finely chopped red onion

¼ cup chopped fresh cilantro

In each individual serving bowl, arrange evenly divided portions of the rice, beans, corn, Pico de Gallo, lettuce, and salmon in a clockwise pattern. Drizzle with the Orange Crema. Garnish with the onion and cilantro.

GRINGO TACOS

"Gringo Taco" is sort of a joke name because a lot of non-Mexicans first started loving tacos thanks to Taco Bell, which for the record did not invent the hard-shell taco filled with spiced ground meat, which is basically what a Gringo Taco is. It's beefy and mildly spicy and really good. Its origins are a little fuzzy but it most likely was first cooked up in Texas, where beef was plentiful and Mexican immigrants made the most of what they had at hand.

Makes 12 tacos

Gringo Seasoning

2 teaspoons onion powder

1½ teaspoons dried red pepper flakes or chopped dried chile de árbol

1 tablespoon chili powder

1½ teaspoons ground cumin

1½ teaspoons sweet paprika

1 teaspoon garlic powder

1 teaspoon dried oregano

2 tablespoons canola oil

1 medium white onion, diced

1½ pounds 80% lean ground beef

1 teaspoon kosher salt

½ teaspoon freshly ground black pepper

12 hard-shell tacos

¼ cup shredded Mexican-style cheese blend, store-bought or homemade (see page 86)

¼ cup shredded iceberg lettuce

Hot sauce, such as Trejo's, Cholula, or Tapatío

1½ cups Pico de Gallo (page 48)

MAKE THE GRINGO SEASONING In a medium bowl, mix the onion powder, red pepper flakes, chili powder, cumin, paprika, garlic powder, and oregano.

COOK THE BEEF Heat the oil in a large skillet over medium-high heat until it is shimmering, about 2 minutes. Add the onion and cook until it is soft and translucent, 5 to 7 minutes. Add the beef and the Gringo Seasoning and cook, stirring occasionally, until the beef is browned, about 15 minutes. Add ½ cup of water and use a wooden spoon to scrape up the bits from the bottom. Cook until most of the water has evaporated, about 5 minutes. Add the salt and pepper and stir to combine. Remove from the heat and set aside to cool.

MAKE THE TACOS Divide the beef among the taco shells, top each taco with the cheese, and then add the lettuce. Serve with hot sauce to taste and the Pico de Gallo.

Grilled Spicy Diablo Shrimp

This is hot and sweet and will blow your head off in the best way. If you don't like your food too spicy, feel free to only use two chipotles.

Serves 4

1 medium head of garlic (about 10 cloves), cloves separated and peeled

½ cup plus 2 tablespoons pure olive oil

4 chipotle chiles from a can of chipotle chiles in adobo sauce, plus 2 tablespoons of the sauce

1 teaspoon garlic powder

¼ cup honey

Juice of 1 lime

¾ teaspoon kosher salt

1 pound jumbo shrimp, peeled and deveined

MAKE THE DIABLO SAUCE Preheat the oven to 350°F. On a rimmed baking sheet, toss the garlic cloves with 2 tablespoons of the olive oil. Bake, stirring midway through, until the garlic is soft and medium brown but not too dark. Check at 30 minutes and, if it's getting too dark, remove. If not, cook for up to 45 minutes.

Place the remaining ½ cup oil, the roasted garlic and oil from the baking sheet, the chiles with the 2 tablespoons adobo sauce, and the garlic powder in a blender and puree. While the blender is running, slowly drizzle in the honey. Add the lime juice and salt, and puree until smooth.

MARINATE THE SHRIMP Transfer the diablo sauce to a large bowl, add the shrimp, and mix until the shrimp are well coated. Place the bowl in the refrigerator and marinate the shrimp for at least 10 minutes and up to 1 hour.

GRILL THE SHRIMP Heat a charcoal or gas grill to medium heat. Place the shrimp on the hot grill and cook until grill marks appear, about 3 minutes. Turn the shrimp over and cook until firm, about 3 minutes more. (Or, if you are cooking them on the stove, preheat 1 tablespoon of neutral oil in a large skillet until it is hot. Add the shrimp and cook until they are firm and lightly caramelized, about 3 minutes per side.)

Serve the shrimp in tacos or burritos.

SPICY DIABLO SHRIMP TACOS

Makes 12 tacos

12 6-inch corn tortillas
1 cup shredded red cabbage
¼ cup Pickled Red Onions (page 50)
½ cup Avocado Crema (page 61)
3 cups Grilled Spicy Diablo Shrimp (page 118)
Finely chopped fresh cilantro
2 limes, each cut into 6 wedges

Preheat the oven to 250°F.

Stack the tortillas, wrap them in aluminum foil, place them in the oven, and let them warm until they're fragrant and pliable, about 15 minutes.

Remove the tortillas from the oven. Unwrap the stack and line up the tortillas, assembly-line-style, on your work surface.

In a medium bowl, stir together the cabbage and pickled onions. Drizzle the Avocado Crema down the center of each tortilla. Place the cabbage-onion slaw in a straight line over the crema and set the shrimp on top of the slaw. Sprinkle with the cilantro and serve with the lime wedges.

SPICY DIABLO SHRIMP BURRITOS

Makes 4 burritos

1 cup shredded red cabbage
½ cup Pickled Red Onions (page 50)
4 13-inch flour tortillas
½ cup shredded Mexican-style cheese blend, store-bought or homemade (see page 86)
1 cup Spanish Rice (page 171), warmed
1 cup Basic Black Beans (page 170), warmed
2 cups Grilled Spicy Diablo Shrimp (page 118)
1 cup Avocado Crema (page 61)
Salsa Roja (page 53), for serving

In a medium bowl, stir together the cabbage and pickled onions.

Place a tortilla in a large skillet set over medium heat, warming it until it is heated through and lightly browned in spots, about 1 minute. Turn the tortilla over and warm it on the second side, 1 minute more. Transfer the tortilla to a plate and cover it with a kitchen towel to keep it warm. Repeat with the remaining tortillas.

Lay the tortillas out on your work surface. Sprinkle 2 tablespoons of the cheese in a straight line across the middle of each tortilla. Layer ¼ cup of the rice, ¼ cup of the beans, and ½ cup of the shrimp on top of the cheese. Top the shrimp with the cabbage-onion mixture. Drizzle the Avocado Crema over the top. Fold the left and right sides of each tortilla in by 1 inch. Grab the bottom of the tortilla and roll it away from you, ensuring the sides are tucked in. Serve with Salsa Roja on the side.

MEXI-FALAFEL TACOS

Hearty Tuscan kale works best in this taco if it is sliced super thin. Remove the fibrous center rib before slicing the leaves.

Makes 12 tacos

¼ cup tahini

2 tablespoons pure olive oil

Juice of 1 lemon

¼ teaspoon ground cumin

¼ teaspoon kosher salt

1 16-ounce box falafel mix, such as Trader Joe's brand

2 cups neutral oil, such as safflower or canola

12 6-inch corn tortillas

1½ cups finely sliced Tuscan kale (from about 4 leaves)

½ cup Pickled Red Onions (page 50)

2 limes, each cut into 6 wedges

In a medium bowl, combine the tahini, olive oil, lemon juice, cumin, salt, and 2 tablespoons of water and stir well. Set aside.

Prepare the falafel mixture according to the package instructions, and then form it into 1-inch balls. Fry the falafel in the oil per the box instructions.

Preheat the oven to 250°F.

Stack the tortillas, wrap them in aluminum foil, place them in the oven, and let them warm until they're fragrant and pliable, about 15 minutes.

Remove the tortillas from the oven. Unwrap the stack and line up the tortillas, assembly-line-style, on your work surface.

Drizzle each tortilla with the tahini sauce in a zigzag pattern. Place the kale in a straight line down the center of each tortilla. Set the falafel balls in a straight line on top of the kale. Top the falafel with the pickled onions and serve a lime wedge with each taco.

JACKFRUIT TACOS

I'm going to sound like a jerk here, but I used to feel sorry for vegans. Owning Trejo's Tacos changed that. While I like to cook, I knew I needed to turn to the professionals to dial in the recipes. When the chefs were creating the taco menu, we knew we wanted vegan options and I thought that might just mean a lot of rice and bean burritos and *papas con rajas* (potato and chile) tacos. One day they presented me with some new menu options and handed me a taco with a savory shredded filling that was spicy and tender. I was like: "What kind of meat is this? It's delicious." They said: "It's jackfruit." I had no idea what jackfruit was, but it turns out it's one of the world's superfoods and grows all over Southeast Asia. It's full of nutrients, and when you cook it in the same marinade we use for our Carne Asada, I swear you'll think it's meat. And if you're vegan you're going to be very, very happy.

Makes 12 tacos

2 9.9-ounce cans jackfruit (about 2 cups)

1½ cups Carne Asada marinade (page 80)

Kosher salt

Freshly ground black pepper

12 6-inch corn tortillas

1 cup shredded red cabbage

1 tablespoon Salsa Verde (page 52; or use store-bought)

¼ cup Avocado Crema (page 61)

1½ cups Pico de Gallo (page 48; or use store-bought)

COOK THE JACKFRUIT Drain the jackfruit and pat it dry with paper towels. In a medium saucepan, stir the jackfruit with the Carne Asada marinade. Set the pan over medium-low heat and cook the jackfruit until it starts to break down and shred, about 45 minutes. Taste and adjust the seasoning with salt and pepper if desired. Remove the pan from the heat.

MAKE THE TACOS Preheat the oven to 250°F. Stack the tortillas, wrap them in aluminum foil, place them in the oven, and let them warm until they're fragrant and pliable, about 15 minutes. Unwrap the stack and line up the tortillas, assembly-line-style, on your work surface. In a small bowl, mix the cabbage with the Salsa Verde and season it to taste with salt and pepper.

Drizzle each tortilla with the Avocado Crema. Place some warm jackfruit in a straight line down the center of each tortilla. Spoon a line of the Salsa Verde slaw on top of the jackfruit, and then top with a line of the Pico de Gallo.

BACON CHEESEBURGER TACOS

L.A. is a burger town. We've got Fatburger, The Apple Pan, and In-N-Out, with its secret menu where all the really good stuff is hidden unless you know what to ask for. And now we've got the Trejo's bacon cheeseburger taco. Who needs a double double animal style when you've got this bacon cheeseburger taco? You won't find this on In-N-Out's secret menu. Yet.

Makes 12 tacos

1 pound 80% lean ground beef

¼ cup Gringo Seasoning (page 116)

2 tablespoons neutral oil, such as canola

12 6-inch corn tortillas

1½ cups shredded Mexican-style cheese blend, store-bought or homemade (see page 86)

¼ cup finely chopped red onion

¼ cup finely chopped fresh cilantro

12 cherry tomatoes, quartered

½ cup roughly chopped crisp-cooked bacon

In a large bowl, combine the ground beef and the Gringo Seasoning, using your hands to evenly distribute the seasoning without overworking the meat. Form the meat into 4 patties, each one about ¾ inch thick.

Heat the oil in a large heavy-bottomed pan or cast-iron skillet over medium-high heat until it is shimmering and just smoking, about 2 minutes. Sear the patties in the hot pan until they are crisp and deeply browned on the bottom, about 5 minutes. Turn the patties over and cook on the other side for 4 minutes for medium doneness. Transfer the patties to a cutting board and let them cool for 5 minutes (you don't want the juices running out and leaving you with dry meat). Then chop the patties into a rough ½-inch dice.

Preheat the oven to 250°F.

Stack the tortillas, wrap them in aluminum foil, place them in the oven, and let them warm until they're fragrant and pliable, about 15 minutes.

Remove the tortillas from the oven. Unwrap the stack and line up the tortillas, assembly-line-style, on your work surface. Place the beef in a straight line down the center of each tortilla. Sprinkle a line of cheese over the beef, then top with onion, cilantro, cherry tomatoes, and bacon, and serve.

Mushroom Asada

We call this vegan filling "asada" even though it's technically not an *asada* (which is Spanish for "grilled"), because it does use the same marinade that goes on our Carne Asada. Mushrooms soak up all the spicy, savory flavors and make a hearty taco filling.

Serves 4 to 6

- 1 pound mushrooms, such as cremini, stemmed and sliced
- 1½ cups Carne Asada marinade (page 80)
- 2 tablespoons pure olive oil

In a medium bowl, toss the mushrooms with the marinade. Set them aside to marinate for 30 minutes.

Set a large skillet over medium-high heat, add the olive oil, and heat until it is shimmering, 2 minutes. Working in batches (if you overcrowd the pan, they will steam instead of brown), cook the mushrooms, stirring often, until they are lightly browned, about 15 minutes per batch.

Serve the mushrooms as tacos or bowls (recipes follow), or with all the fixings for Carne Asada Tacos (page 82), or swap them in for the chicken on Pollo Frito Quesadillas (page 147).

MUSHROOM ASADA TACOS

Makes 12 tacos

12 6-inch corn tortillas
1½ cups shredded green cabbage
¼ cup Salsa Verde (page 52)
1 recipe Mushroom Asada (page 128)
½ cup Pepita Pesto (page 56)
3 limes, quartered (12 wedges)

Preheat the oven to 250°F.

Stack the tortillas, wrap them in aluminum foil, place them in the oven, and let them warm until they're fragrant and pliable, about 15 minutes.

Remove the tortillas from the oven. Unwrap the stack and line up the tortillas, assembly-line-style, on your work surface.

In a medium bowl, mix the shredded cabbage with the Salsa Verde. Spoon the mushrooms in a straight line down the center of each tortilla. Place a line of the cabbage mixture on top of the mushrooms, and top that with the pesto. Serve each taco with a lime wedge.

MUSHROOM ASADA BOWLS

Makes 4 bowls

2 cups Spanish Rice (page 171), warmed
2 cups Basic Black Beans (page 170), warmed
2 cups grilled corn (see page 163)
1 cup Pico de Gallo (page 48)
1 cup shredded romaine lettuce
1 recipe Mushroom Asada (page 128)
½ cup Pepita Pesto (page 56)

In each individual serving bowl, arrange evenly divided portions of the rice, beans, corn, Pico de Gallo, lettuce, and Mushroom Asada in a clockwise pattern. Top with the Pepita Pesto.

BREAKFAST BURRITO

We serve this all day long because it's just that damned good. It has everything you want for breakfast, plus tater tots. It's even better if you've got some left-over Carne Asada (page 80) or Carnitas (page 84).

Makes 4 burritos

24 frozen tater tots

1 tablespoon canola or vegetable oil

8 large eggs, whisked

Kosher salt

Freshly ground black pepper

4 13-inch flour tortillas

½ cup shredded Mexican-style cheese blend, store-bought or homemade (see page 86)

1 cup Cheesy Bean Dip (page 63), warmed

4 bacon strips, cooked until crisp

1 avocado, halved, pitted, peeled, and sliced (optional)

½ cup Salsa Roja (page 53) or store-bought fire-roasted tomato salsa, plus extra for serving

½ cup tortilla strips (see page 77) or crumbled tortilla chips

½ cup chopped fresh cilantro

Cook the tater tots according to the package directions. (We fry them to order at the restaurant; you can do that, or bake them—they're almost just as good!)

Heat the oil in a large pan set over medium heat. Add the eggs and season with salt and pepper. Using a fork (or a silicone spatula if you're using a nonstick pan), constantly stir the eggs in a figure-eight pattern, taking care to scrape up any bits that are getting too firm or are sticking to the pan. Continue stirring the eggs until they are cooked through but still slightly wet, about 4 minutes. Season with a bit more salt and pepper. Set the pan of eggs aside.

Place a tortilla in a large skillet set over medium heat, warming it until it is heated through and lightly browned in spots, about 1 minute. Turn the tortilla over and warm it on the second side, 1 minute more. Transfer the tortilla to a plate and cover it with a kitchen towel to keep it warm. Repeat with the remaining tortillas.

Lay the tortillas out on your work surface. Sprinkle the cheese across the middle of each tortilla. Layer ¼ cup of the bean dip over the cheese and add 5 or 6 tater tots to the side. Add the eggs to the center, 1 strip of bacon to the side of the eggs, and a few slices of avocado, if using. Finish with the Salsa Roja, tortilla strips, and cilantro. Fold the left and right sides of each tortilla in by 1 inch. Grab the bottom of the tortilla and roll it away from you, ensuring the sides are tucked in. Serve with more Salsa Roja on the side.

SURF & TURF BURRITOS

Is a surf and turf burrito overkill? Perhaps, but in the best way possible. If you've got leftover *asada*, you're living large, because you can just cook up some marinated shrimp to make the richest burrito we've got on the menu. You'll notice this is a pretty elaborate setup, with nutty Pepita Pesto, fresh Pico de Gallo, spicy Salsa Roja, and black beans tucked inside the tortilla. If you want to make a shortcut version, you can ditch the homemade salsas and use store-bought fire-roasted tomato salsa, skip the rice and beans, and just cook up some plain shrimp because when you have steak and shrimp side by side, you can't go wrong.

Makes 4 burritos

1 tablespoon canola or vegetable oil

12 marinated Spicy Diablo Shrimp (page 118), or 12 medium shrimp, peeled and deveined

1 garlic clove, chopped

Kosher salt

Freshly ground black pepper

4 13-inch flour tortillas

½ cup shredded Mexican-style cheese blend, store-bought or homemade (see page 86)

1 cup Spanish Rice (page 171), warmed

1 cup canned black beans, rinsed and drained, or Basic Black Beans (page 170), warmed

½ cup chopped Carne Asada (page 80), warmed

¼ cup Pepita Pesto (page 56)

½ cup Pico de Gallo (page 48)

Salsa Roja (page 53), for serving

Heat the oil in a medium skillet set over medium heat until it is shimmering, about 2 minutes. Add the shrimp and garlic and cook, stirring often, until the garlic is fragrant and the shrimp is cooked through, about 5 minutes. Season to taste with salt and pepper. Transfer the shrimp to a cutting board and chop it into ½-inch pieces.

Place a tortilla in a large skillet set over medium heat, warming it until it is heated through and lightly browned in spots, about 1 minute. Turn the tortilla over and warm it on the second side, 1 minute more. Transfer the tortilla to a plate and cover it with a kitchen towel to keep it warm. Repeat with the remaining tortillas.

Lay the tortillas out on your work surface. Sprinkle 2 tablespoons of the cheese in a straight line across the middle of each tortilla. Layer ¼ cup of the rice, ¼ cup of the beans, 2 tablespoons of the Carne Asada, and ½ cup of the shrimp over the cheese. Top with the Pepita Pesto and Pico de Gallo. Fold the left and right sides of each tortilla in by 1 inch. Grab the bottom of the tortilla and roll it away from you, ensuring the sides are tucked in. Serve with Salsa Roja on the side.

ROASTED CAULIFLOWER TACOS

I never thought I'd see the day that cauliflower was put on a taco, but this is California, so why not? I was skeptical. And then I tasted what our chefs did with it. It's unbelievably tender and tasty, and the cashew cream makes it rich and satisfying. This is the taco that the *Los Angeles Times* called one of their favorite recipes of 2017. It's vegan! It's delicious!

Makes 8 tacos

1 medium head cauliflower

2 tablespoons pure olive oil

1 teaspoon kosher salt

1 teaspoon freshly ground black pepper

1 ear corn, shucked

8 6-inch corn tortillas

½ cup Vegan Cashew Crema (page 59)

½ cup Pickled Red Onions (page 50)

¼ cup chopped fresh cilantro

ROAST THE CAULIFLOWER Preheat the oven to 375°F.

Remove the cauliflower florets from the thick stem and break the florets into bite-sized pieces. Scatter the cauliflower florets on a rimmed 11 x 17-inch sheet pan, drizzle with the oil, season with the salt and pepper, and toss to coat. Roast the cauliflower until it is tender, about 30 minutes. Then raise the heat to 425°F and continue to cook until the cauliflower is lightly browned, about 10 minutes more. Set aside.

CHAR THE CORN While the cauliflower is cooking, turn a gas burner to high and place the ear of corn directly on the rack over the flame. (If you don't have a gas oven, you can broil the corn.) Cook until the corn is charred in spots, turning it occasionally with tongs, about 2 minutes per side. Set the ear of corn aside to cool until you can handle it.

In a medium mixing bowl, hold the ear of corn vertically and slice downward on each side to remove the kernels, letting them fall into the bowl. Discard the cob and use your hands to break the clumps of corn into separate kernels. Set aside.

MAKE THE TACOS Preheat the oven to 250°F.

Stack the tortillas, wrap them in aluminum foil, place them in the oven, and let them warm until they're fragrant and pliable, about 15 minutes.

Remove the tortillas from the oven. Unwrap the stack and line up the tortillas, assembly-line-style, on your work surface.

Spoon 1 tablespoon of the Vegan Cashew Crema in the center of each tortilla. Place several florets of roasted cauliflower on top of the crema and top them with some corn. Drizzle with more crema and garnish with the pickled onions and chopped cilantro.

ROASTED CAULIFLOWER BOWLS

Makes 4 bowls

2 cups Spanish Rice (page 171), warmed

2 cups Basic Black Beans (page 170), warmed

2 cups grilled corn (see page 163)

1 cup Pico de Gallo (page 48)

1 cup shredded romaine lettuce

2 cups roasted cauliflower florets (see page 136)

½ cup Vegan Cashew Crema (page 59)

¼ cup chopped red onion

¼ cup chopped fresh cilantro

½ cup Pickled Red Onions (page 50)

In each individual serving bowl, arrange evenly divided portions of the rice, beans, corn, Pico de Gallo, lettuce, and cauliflower in a clockwise pattern. Drizzle with the Vegan Cashew Crema. Garnish with the onion, cilantro, and pickled onions.

BCR (BEAN, CHEESE & RICE) BURRITOS

This is the cheapest burrito on our menu, but it has tons of flavor thanks to the power of the Cheesy Bean Dip. We mix in some black beans to cut the richness just a little bit. It's also vegetarian.

Makes 4 burritos

4 13-inch flour tortillas

1 cup Cheesy Bean Dip (page 63), warmed

1 cup shredded Mexican-style cheese blend, store-bought or homemade (see page 86)

1 cup Basic Black Beans (page 170), warmed

1 cup Spanish Rice (page 171), warmed

Salsa Roja (page 53), for serving

Place a tortilla in a large skillet set over medium heat, warming it until it is heated through and lightly browned in spots, about 1 minute. Turn the tortilla over and warm it on the second side, 1 minute more. Transfer the tortilla to a plate and cover it with a kitchen towel to keep it warm. Repeat with the remaining tortillas.

Lay the tortillas out on your work surface. Spread ¼ cup of the Cheesy Bean Dip in a straight line across the center of each tortilla. Layer ¼ cup of the cheese, ¼ cup of the black beans, and ¼ cup of the rice on top of the Cheesy Bean Dip. Fold the left and right sides of each tortilla in by 1 inch. Grab the bottom of the tortilla and roll it away from you, ensuring the sides are tucked in. Serve with Salsa Roja.

FRIED AVOCADO TACOS

Avocado toast has nothing on these tacos. Because you can't fry avocado toast! The crunchy exterior and creamy inside of this taco is unexpectedly satisfying. It's rich and, yes, vegetarian. So they're good . . . but they're fried. So they're bad? The duality! This is another multistep frying project that pays off big-time.

Makes 8 tacos

2 large eggs, beaten

1½ cups panko bread crumbs

1 cup rice flour

2 avocados, halved, pitted, and peeled

Kosher salt

4 cups peanut oil

8 6-inch corn tortillas

1 cup Refried Black Beans (page 173), warmed

1 cup shredded romaine lettuce

½ cup Salsa Verde (page 52)

½ cup Pico de Gallo (page 48), plus extra for garnish

¼ cup finely chopped fresh cilantro

BREAD AND FRY THE AVOCADOS Set up your frying station: Add the eggs to a medium bowl, the panko to another, and the flour to a third. Slice each avocado half lengthwise into 8 pieces, and season the pieces with salt.

In a large deep pot, heat the oil until it reaches 350°F on an instant-read thermometer.

While the oil is heating, bread the avocado: Dredge the avocado slices in the flour first, shaking the excess back into the bowl. Then dip the slices in the egg, making sure to coat them completely and allowing the excess to drip back into the bowl. Finally dredge the avocado slices in the panko, pressing gently so it adheres. Place the breaded slices on a plate. (Use one hand for dredging and dipping to keep the other hand clean for other tasks.)

Fry the avocado, 6 to 8 slices at a time (you don't want to overcrowd the pot), in the hot oil, turning them occasionally, until they are golden brown and crisp, 3 to 4 minutes. Transfer the slices to a wire rack or a plate lined with paper towels to drain, and season them liberally with salt.

MAKE THE TACOS Preheat the oven to 250°F.

Stack the tortillas, wrap them in aluminum foil, place them in the oven, and let them warm until they're fragrant and pliable, about 15 minutes.

Remove the tortillas from the oven. Unwrap the stack and line up the tortillas, assembly-line-style, on your work surface.

On each of the tortillas, spread 2 tablespoons of the beans. Then top the beans with the lettuce, Salsa Verde, and Pico de Gallo. Place 4 pieces of avocado on top. Garnish with a little more Pico de Gallo and the cilantro.

BLACK PEPPER TOFU TACOS

This vegan taco is rich, spicy, and intensely flavored with fresh ginger and fiery serrano chiles, which makes it as satisfying as any meat taco on our menu. Yes, it's fried, which is part of the reason why it's so damned good. Just because something's vegan doesn't mean it's healthy (or boring)! The trick to getting the fragile tofu to hold together is to fry it in small batches and gently remove it from the oil using a frying spider or a fine-mesh sieve. Top the tofu with the sauce once it's in the taco—or serve the tofu and sauce over steamed rice.

Makes 12 tacos

- 1¾ pounds firm tofu (a little less than 2 14-ounce blocks)
- ½ cup cornstarch
- 2 cups plus 2 tablespoons canola oil
- 8 medium shallots, halved and thinly sliced
- 8 garlic cloves, finely chopped
- 2 serrano chiles, stemmed and thinly sliced crosswise
- 3 tablespoons finely chopped fresh ginger
- 3 tablespoons chopped chipotles from a can of chipotle chiles in adobo sauce
- 3 tablespoons low-sodium soy sauce
- 2 tablespoons sugar
- 2 tablespoons freshly ground black pepper
- 1 teaspoon kosher salt
- 3 scallions, finely chopped
- 12 6-inch corn tortillas
- 1 medium white onion, diced
- ¼ cup finely chopped fresh cilantro
- 1 cup Salsa Roja (page 53)

It's important to get as much water out of the tofu as possible before cooking it. To do this, place the tofu on a plate and then balance another plate on top and weight it down with any canned food you have in your cupboard (a big can of tomatoes works well). Let it sit for 30 minutes or so, occasionally draining off the water that the tofu releases. Pat the tofu dry with a paper towel, and dice it into 1-inch cubes.

Set up your frying station: Place the cornstarch in a medium bowl. Line a large plate with paper towels.

Heat 2 cups of the oil in a large deep saucepan over medium heat until the oil reaches 350°F on an instant-read thermometer. Add about one-third of the tofu to the cornstarch and use a fork to turn it in the cornstarch, making sure it's well coated on all sides. Add the cornstarch-coated tofu to the hot oil and fry until it is lightly browned all over, using a frying spider or slotted spoon to turn it occasionally, about 3 minutes per side. Transfer the tofu to the plate lined with paper towels to drain. Repeat with the remaining tofu in two more batches.

Heat the remaining 2 tablespoons oil in a large skillet over medium-high heat until it is shimmering. Add the shallots, garlic, serrano chiles, and ginger and cook, stirring often, until they are soft and slightly caramelized, 7 to 10 minutes. Stir in the chipotle chiles, soy sauce, sugar, pepper, and salt. Add the tofu to the skillet and cook, stirring gently, until it is warmed through, about 2 minutes. Add the scallions and gently fold them in, taking care to not break up the tofu. Set aside.

Preheat the oven to 250°F.

Wrap the tortillas in aluminum foil, place them in the oven, and let them warm until they're fragrant and pliable, about 15 minutes.

Remove the tortillas from the oven. Unwrap the stack and line up the tortillas, assembly-line-style, on your work surface. Divide the tofu evenly among the tortillas and top it with the onion and cilantro. Serve with the Salsa Roja on the side.

Trejo's Tip

OVERCOME YOUR FEAR OF FRYING

Frying can seem intimidating at first. But the trick is to be organized; have your ingredients prepared, have the right equipment laid out and ready, and have the oil temperature set to just the right heat. If you have a deep fryer with temperature controls and a basket, great — that takes care of most of that. But if you don't, be sure to fry in a deep pot, and never fill the pot more than halfway with oil. You don't want the oil boiling over and onto your burner! You'll also want what's called a spider strainer (or frying spider), a tool with a long handle and a metal basket at the end for removing food from the oil. A candy thermometer, deep-frying thermometer, or instant-read thermometer will help to monitor the temperature. For frying, 350°F is the magic number: it's hot enough to cook whatever you're frying all the way through and give it that perfect golden-brown crust without burning it.

KILLER QUESADILLAS

It might seem ridiculous to offer recipes for something as simple as a quesadilla, but they're one of the most popular items on our menu, so we have to be doing something right. When my kids were little I'd just throw quesadillas together without really thinking about it, but at the restaurants ours are consistently delicious because of the proportion of cheese (1 cup for each tortilla is just cheesy enough), the method (pan-toasting both sides of the tortilla), and the fillings and sauces (we pair meats, cremas, and salsas with the same care as we do for our tacos). This "killer" quesadilla is the house recipe we use as the foundation and then add whatever protein is asked for, be it steak, grilled chicken, spicy shrimp, or carnitas. The quesadillas that follow on pages 146 and 147 are more "specialty" quesadillas, but honestly, it's tough to beat the simple pleasures of melty cheese in a toasty tortilla.

This recipe makes two quesadillas but can easily be doubled. If you're making more than two quesadillas, preheat your oven to 250°F to keep the first quesadillas warm while you finish the others.

Makes 2 quesadillas

2 13-inch flour tortillas

2 cups shredded Mexican-style cheese blend, store-bought or homemade (see page 86)

Optional additions: 1½ cups chopped Carne Asada (page 80), Trejo's Grilled Chicken (page 94), Grilled Spicy Diablo Shrimp (page 118), or Carnitas (page 84)

½ cup Salsa Roja (page 53)

Heat a large pan or cast-iron skillet over medium-high heat for 2 minutes. Place a tortilla in the pan and cook until it is lightly browned, about 30 seconds. Turn the tortilla over, spread 1 cup of the cheese evenly across the tortilla, then spread half of your choice of protein, if using, across the tortilla, and cook until the cheese begins to melt, about 3 minutes.

Fold the tortilla in half and cook for 45 seconds. Turn the quesadilla over and cook for another 45 seconds. Transfer it to a cutting board and slice it into 4 wedges.

Repeat with the remaining tortilla and fillings. Serve with Salsa Roja on the side.

CHICKEN TIKKA QUESADILLAS

This quesadilla is a good reason to make a double batch of Chicken Tikka: serve chicken tikka bowls or tacos for dinner one night and have these quesadillas for lunch the next day. The quesadillas get an extra hit of freshness from a mixture of Pico de Gallo and white onion, and we serve it with an escabeche-mint cream on the side—both of which you will have made for the tacos already.

Makes 2 quesadillas

¼ cup Pico de Gallo (page 48)

¼ medium white onion, chopped

2 13-inch flour tortillas

2 cups shredded Mexican-style cheese blend, store-bought or homemade (see page 86)

1½ cups chopped cooked Chicken Tikka (about one-third of the recipe on page 88)

1 cup Escabeche-Mint Crema (page 58)

In a small bowl, combine the Pico de Gallo and onion and mix well.

Heat a large pan or cast-iron skillet over medium-high heat. Place a tortilla in the pan and cook until it is lightly browned, about 30 seconds. Turn the tortilla over and spread 1 cup of the cheese evenly over the top. Sprinkle the Chicken Tikka over the cheese, then spoon the Pico/onion mixture over the chicken. Cook until the cheese begins to melt, about 3 minutes.

Fold the tortilla in half and cook for 45 seconds, then turn the quesadilla over and cook for another 45 seconds on the other side. Transfer the quesadilla to a cutting board and cut it into 4 wedges.

Repeat with the remaining tortilla and fillings. Serve with the Escabeche-Mint Crema on the side.

POLLO FRITO QUESADILLAS

Our fried chicken is killer, and when you add cheesy-toasty-tortilla goodness to it in a quesadilla format, it becomes *even more* satisfying. If you've got any leftover takeout fried chicken, now you know what to do with it.

Makes 2 quesadillas

½ cup shredded green cabbage

½ cup Chipotle Crema (page 60)

2 13-inch flour tortillas

2 cups shredded Mexican-style cheese blend, store-bought or homemade (see page 86)

1½ cups chopped Trejo's Fried Chicken (about one-third of the recipe on page 98)

2 serrano chiles, finely chopped

In a medium bowl, combine the cabbage and ¼ cup of the Chipotle Crema and mix well.

Heat a large pan or cast-iron skillet over medium-high heat. Place a tortilla in the pan and cook until it is lightly browned, about 30 seconds. Turn the tortilla over and spread 1 cup of the cheese evenly across the top, then add ¾ cup of the fried chicken evenly across the tortilla. Sprinkle half of the cabbage mixture over the chicken and then sprinkle half of the serranos evenly on top. Cook until the cheese begins to melt, about 3 minutes.

Fold the tortilla in half and cook for 45 seconds, then turn the quesadilla over and cook for another 45 seconds. Transfer the quesadilla to a cutting board and cut it into 4 wedges.

Repeat with the remaining tortilla and fillings. Serve with the remaining Chipotle Crema on the side.

Ex-cons make the best restaurant reviewers. When we opened the first couple of restaurants, I sent a lot of my old buddies from prison to check them out. The first thing they'd ask me was "Do you want me to wear a wire?" Now these are good guys who had a bad start, guys who cleaned up and straightened out. One was an old workout buddy from my Muscle Beach days (page 42), a guy named Craig Monson. He's a big dude, former Mister World, the first big African-American bodybuilding star. We both did time in San Quentin and would work out together in the yard. When we opened the Cantina in Hollywood, I asked Craig to go in and give me an honest assessment of the restaurant. He went over and looked around: he saw the hostess station, all the original art, the big wraparound bar with the TVs on the wall behind it, the warm tortilla chips and fresh salsa and big trays of beautifully plated food. He came back with his report and I think he said it best: "That ain't no f****n' taco stand, that's a restaurant."

Over the years we've served a lot of food that doesn't fall into the category of taco, burrito, or quesadilla. The recipes in this chapter are basically a grab bag of food that isn't tacos but that is Trejo's through and through—these are the dishes that make our cantinas a serious step up from a taco stand. It's a mix of some basics, like our guacamole (page 152) and street corn (page 166), and some more upscale dishes, like ceviche (page 154), that appear on the menu from time to time. If you want a classic steak, you're going to need to go to a classic steakhouse (see page 39). But when we have a steak on our menu, it comes with a steak sauce spiked with chipotle and lime (page 54) and a side of super-creamy mashed potatoes with roasted poblanos and Mexican cheese mixed in (page 168). It's in the old-school meat and potatoes L.A. steakhouse tradition but with a Mexican twist. That's Trejo's. But so is our El Jefe Salad (page 161), which is in the L.A. tradition of healthy food in that it's made with kale. But we've also loaded it with guacamole and Cotija cheese and roasted corn. It's one of my favorite dishes on the menu. I'm living proof that real men eat kale salad. I have learned to love it. Even though you might know and love us for our tacos, I think you'll fall in love with these recipes, too.

GUACAMOLE

Our guacamole is special because it's got so much more going on than your usual guac. Instead of smashing the avocados, we push them through a checkered wire rack that chefs usually use to cool baked goods. This cubes the avocados without mashing them too much, and then we add pistachios for extra crunch and a little nutty taste. We don't expect you to go out and buy a wire rack, so we've modified this recipe to achieve a similar result. Alongside, we serve chips made by Angeleno tortilla company La Fortaleza. At Trejo's we make a point to support locally owned businesses, so while it might be easy to buy some big-name brand at a supermarket, we suggest you try to find a local tortilla chip maker and keep your money in the community.

Serves 6

3 ripe medium avocados, halved and pitted

½ small white onion, finely chopped

½ serrano or jalapeño chile, finely chopped

4 tablespoons chopped fresh cilantro

Juice of 1 lime, plus extra to taste

1 tablespoon pure olive oil

1 teaspoon kosher salt, plus extra to taste

2 tablespoons chopped salted roasted pistachios

Use a spoon to scoop half of the avocado flesh into a medium bowl. Smash the avocado with a fork or a potato masher until it is mostly smooth.

In a separate medium bowl, lightly mash the remaining avocado so that it's more chunky than smooth. Add the smashed avocado, onion, chile, 2 tablespoons of the cilantro, and the lime juice, olive oil, and salt, and gently fold to combine. Taste and add more lime juice or salt if desired. Serve the guacamole sprinkled with the pistachios and the remaining 2 tablespoons cilantro.

SHRIMP & SCALLOP CEVICHE

Many people are intimidated by the idea of making ceviche at home, but it's incredibly easy, as long as you're cool with squeezing a bunch of citrus! You could use a hinged squeezer and give your forearms a workout, but if you have an electric juicer, this is the time to break it out. One batch of the citrus juice "cooks" the seafood with its acidity, while more juice is added to the aquachile dressing to finish the ceviche with a second layer of fresh flavor.

Serves 6

Ceviche

1 pound large shrimp, peeled, deveined, and chopped into ½-inch pieces

½ pound bay scallops

2 cups fresh lime juice (from about 12 to 14 limes)

Aquachile Dressing

2 scallions, white and green parts, chopped

1 Persian cucumber, roughly chopped

1 jalapeño, roughly chopped

¾ cup roughly chopped fresh cilantro

½ medium serrano chile, roughly chopped

¼ cup roughly chopped fresh flat-leaf parsley

⅓ cup lemon juice (from about 3 lemons)

¼ cup lime juice (from about 2 limes)

1 teaspoon kosher salt

Garnish

½ medium red onion, diced

1 small Persian cucumber, diced

¼ cup diced grilled pineapple (see page 86; optional)

3 tablespoons Pico de Gallo (page 48)

1 tablespoon chopped fresh cilantro

"COOK" THE CEVICHE In a large bowl, combine the shrimp, scallops, and lime juice. Cover the bowl with plastic wrap and refrigerate for 3 hours.

MAKE THE AGUACHILE DRESSING Put the scallions, cucumber, jalapeño, cilantro, serrano, parsley, lemon juice, lime juice, and salt in a blender and blend until smooth.

FINISH THE CEVICHE When the shrimp and scallops are done "cooking" (they will firm up and turn from translucent to white), drain them and return them to the bowl. Add the aguachile dressing, and mix together.

Transfer the ceviche to a serving platter and garnish it with the diced onion, cucumber, pineapple, if using, Pico de Gallo, and cilantro.

Trejo's Tip

SERVING CEVICHE

You can serve this ceviche on tostadas (see page 104) or with store-bought tortilla chips.

TREJO'S CHICKEN WINGS WITH BLUE CHEESE DIP

These wings have a lot in common with Buffalo wings, except you don't have to fry them and you use a good old Mexican hot sauce instead of the traditional Frank's Hot Sauce that they use in New York. Not frying means you've got more time to watch the game and don't have to worry about one of your friends knocking the hot oil all over the place when your team scores. Make the dip a day or two before the game so you'll have it ready when the wings come out of the oven.

Serves 4 to 6 (makes 2 cups dip)

Wings

- 1 tablespoon baking powder
- 1 teaspoon garlic powder
- 1 teaspoon onion powder
- 1 teaspoon cayenne pepper
- 1 teaspoon paprika
- 2 pounds chicken wings (about 20 pieces), cut into drumettes and flats, patted dry with paper towels
- 1 tablespoon canola oil
- 4 tablespoons (½ stick) unsalted butter, melted
- 2 tablespoons hot sauce, such as Trejo's, Tapatío, or Cholula

Blue Cheese Dip

- 1 cup crumbled blue cheese
- ½ cup sour cream
- ¼ cup mayonnaise
- Juice of ½ lemon
- 1 tablespoon whole milk or buttermilk
- 1 small garlic clove, chopped
- Kosher salt
- Freshly ground black pepper

ROAST THE WINGS Preheat the oven to 400°F.

In a large bowl, combine the baking powder, garlic powder, onion powder, cayenne, and paprika. Add the wings and stir to coat them.

Line an 11 x 17-inch sheet pan with aluminum foil. Use the canola oil to grease the foil and then turn the wings out onto the pan. Roast the wings until they're golden brown, about 45 minutes.

MAKE THE DIP   In a medium bowl, whisk together the blue cheese, sour cream, mayonnaise, lemon juice, milk, garlic, and a few pinches each of salt and pepper. Stir to combine, then taste and add more salt or pepper if needed. Serve immediately, or cover the bowl with plastic wrap and refrigerate it for up to 3 days.

SAUCE THE WINGS   In a small bowl, whisk together the melted butter and the hot sauce. As soon as the wings come out of the oven, pour the spicy butter sauce over them and toss to coat. Serve with the blue cheese dip.

NACHOS

The difference between a good plate of nachos and a great plate of nachos is the placement of all the ingredients. You want to make sure you get everything evenly spread out in and around and on each chip, so every bite's got the melty cheese, a bit of jalapeño, some beans, and some of our killer Chipotle Crema.

Serves 4

4 cups tortilla chips

1 cup shredded Mexican-style cheese blend, store-bought or homemade (see page 86)

1 cup canned black or pinto beans, drained and rinsed, or 1 cup leftover Basic Black Beans (page 170), warmed

1 cup Pico de Gallo (page 48)

¼ cup Chipotle Crema (page 60)

½ cup Escabeche (page 51) or canned pickled jalapeños, drained

2 tablespoons crumbled Cotija cheese

2 tablespoons finely chopped fresh cilantro

Preheat the oven to 350°F.

Scatter the tortilla chips on a sheet pan and sprinkle them evenly with the shredded cheese, making sure each chip has some cheese on it. Bake until the cheese is melted, 3 to 5 minutes.

Top the chips with the beans and Pico de Gallo. Drizzle with the Chipotle Crema. Sprinkle the Escabeche over the chips, followed by the Cotija and cilantro, and serve.

FAJITAS

Fajitas aren't an L.A. dish, but we included them on our menu because sometimes people don't want superspicy Mexican food. This dish has its roots in Texas, where gauchos would cook up beef with whatever vegetables were handy. Our version isn't fancy, but it's a satisfying throwback to a dish that's not as trendy as it used to be. Use whatever protein you want. If you don't serve it with rice or tortillas, it's technically paleo, which appeals to the bodybuilder in me.

Serves 4

3 tablespoons pure olive oil

1 large white onion, halved lengthwise and thinly sliced

1 red bell pepper, halved, seeded, and sliced into thin strips

1 yellow bell pepper, halved, seeded, and sliced into thin strips

2 poblano peppers, halved, seeded, and sliced into thin strips

Kosher salt

Freshly ground black pepper

1½ pounds protein of your choice (skirt steak; boneless, skinless chicken thighs or breasts; peeled and deveined medium shrimp; tofu)

3 garlic cloves, minced

1 lime, cut into 4 wedges

8 10-inch flour tortillas, warmed (see page 78)

Store-bought roasted tomato salsa or salsa verde, or homemade Salsa Roja (page 53) or Salsa Verde (page 52), for serving

In a cast-iron skillet, heat 2 tablespoons of the oil over high heat. Add the onion and the red, yellow, and poblano peppers. Season with salt and pepper and cook, stirring often, until the vegetables are soft and lightly browned in spots, about 7 minutes. Transfer them to a plate and set aside.

Add the remaining 1 tablespoon oil, along with the protein and garlic to the skillet, and cook until the protein is browned and cooked through on both sides: 3 minutes per side for skirt steak; 5 minutes per side for chicken breasts; 8 minutes per side for chicken thighs; 2 minutes per side for shrimp; 3 minutes per side for tofu. If you are using steak or chicken, transfer it to a cutting board and let it rest for 5 minutes before slicing it crosswise into thin strips. Reserve the skillet.

Return the vegetable mixture to the skillet and reheat it over high heat, tossing it with the juices in the skillet. Divide the mixture among individual plates and top it with the protein. Serve with the lime wedges, warm tortillas, and your favorite salsa.

EL JEFE SALAD

This chopped salad is pretty much the opposite of nachos on the healthy spectrum. But it's still crunchy, bright, and satisfying. Top the salad with any of the proteins in this book and you've got yourself a meal.

Serves 4

3 tablespoons pure olive oil

Juice of 1 lemon

Juice of ½ lime

Kosher salt

Freshly ground black pepper

4 medium leaves Tuscan black kale, stems removed, leaves finely chopped (about 1 cup)

1 small head romaine lettuce, very thinly sliced (about 4 cups)

½ cup roasted corn (see page 163)

½ cup canned black beans, drained and rinsed, or ½ cup Basic Black Beans (page 170)

½ cup quartered cherry tomatoes

¼ cup crumbled Cotija cheese

¼ cup Guacamole (page 152)

1 cup grilled shrimp, chicken, *asada*, or *carnitas* (optional)

½ cup tortilla strips (see page 77)

In a large bowl, whisk together the olive oil, lemon and lime juices, and salt and pepper to taste until combined. Add the kale and the lettuce, and toss the greens with the vinaigrette. Top with the corn, black beans, cherry tomatoes, and Cotija.

Place the guacamole on one side of the bowl and the protein, if using, across from it. Garnish with the tortilla strips and serve.

KALE SALAD

I'm not ashamed to say I eat kale salad. In fact, I've appeared on national TV eating kale salad in an episode of the late and great Anthony Bourdain's *Parts Unknown*! Kale is sturdy enough that it won't wilt over time, making this an excellent salad to put together in advance for a party.

Serves 4

2 medium bunches Tuscan kale, tough stems removed and leaves sliced into thin ribbons (6 cups)

½ small cucumber, diced

½ small red bell pepper, diced

½ cup canned black beans, drained and rinsed, or ½ cup Basic Black Beans (page 170)

½ cup halved cherry tomatoes

½ cup roasted corn (see sidebar, opposite)

1 teaspoon kosher salt

¼ cup Creamy Cilantro-Lime Vinaigrette (page 58)

2 tablespoons toasted pepitas

1 lemon, cut into 4 wedges

In a medium bowl, toss together the kale, cucumber, bell pepper, black beans, tomatoes, corn, and salt. Add the vinaigrette and mix well to combine. Divide the salad among individual bowls and sprinkle with the pepitas. Serve with the lemon wedges on the side.

HOW TO
ROAST CORN

There's no single best way to roast corn. Each technique has a slightly different outcome. Pan roasting yields a drier but more intensely flavored corn kernel; grilling adds smoke and sweetness; stove-top charring cooks the corn quickly, so the kernels stay milky and juicy while also delivering a nice balance of fresh/sweet and roasted/smoky.

PAN ROASTING Stand each ear of corn upright on a cutting board or in a bowl, and slice from top to bottom to cut the kernels off the cob. In a medium cast-iron pan, cook the corn kernels over medium-high heat, stirring occasionally, until they are browned and toasted, 5 to 7 minutes.

GRILLING On a grill at medium heat, grill the husked ears of corn, turning them every few minutes, until the kernels are blistered and their color has gone from pale to bright yellow. Let the ears cool and then slice the kernels off the cobs.

STOVETOP CHARRING Set a husked ear of corn directly on your stovetop's burner (you need a gas burner for this method). Using tongs, turn the ear of corn every few minutes, cooking until the tips of most of the kernels are blistered, about 5 minutes total. Let the corn cool, and then slice the kernels off the cob.

ROASTED BRUSSELS SPROUTS
WITH RED CHIMICHURRI

When I was growing up, nobody liked to eat their brussels sprouts, so I was skeptical when the chefs wanted to put sprouts on the menu at Trejo's. I've since learned that back in the day, nobody knew how to cook them. People used to boil them too long, which made them taste like sulfur. But then somebody figured out that you should roast the heck out of them, caramelize them, and make them toasty and tender. And now everybody loves them, including me. We deep-fry the brussels sprouts at the restaurant, which is insanely delicious but scary as hell. Roasting is healthier and way less scary.

The red chimichurri is different from the usual green version, thanks to smoked paprika and chipotle chili. It's spicy, tangy, and smoky and is great on broccoli and cauliflower and all those other vegetables we used to hate but now love when they're roasted the right way.

Serves 4 (makes ¾ cup chimichurri)

Brussels Sprouts

1½ pounds brussels sprouts, stem ends trimmed, halved lengthwise

¼ cup pure olive oil

1 teaspoon kosher salt

1 teaspoon freshly ground black pepper

Red Chimichurri

½ cup extra-virgin olive oil

¼ cup red wine vinegar

3 garlic cloves, finely chopped

1 chipotle chile from a can of chipotle chiles in adobo sauce, chopped (about 1 tablespoon)

1 teaspoon smoked paprika

Kosher salt

Freshly ground black pepper

1 cup finely chopped fresh flat-leaf parsley

2 tablespoons finely chopped fresh cilantro

ROAST THE BRUSSELS SPROUTS Preheat the oven to 450°F.

Scatter the brussels sprouts on a rimmed 11 x 17-inch sheet pan and add the oil, salt, and pepper. Toss to coat. Roast the brussels sprouts until they are tender and brown, 20 to 25 minutes.

MAKE THE RED CHIMICHURRI In a large bowl, whisk together the olive oil, vinegar, garlic, chipotle chile, paprika, and salt and pepper to taste. Add the parsley and cilantro and stir to combine.

Add the roasted brussels sprouts to the chimichurri and toss to coat. Transfer

STREET CORN ON THE COB (ELOTE)

On street corners throughout L.A., you'll find push-carts where you can buy *elote* on a stick for 2 bucks. We swap out the mayo a lot of the vendors use for our Chipotle Crema, which makes ours just a little more artisanal . . . but it's still just as satisfying.

Makes 6 pieces

3 ears corn, husked

1 cup crumbled Cotija cheese

1½ cups Chipotle Crema (page 60)

Tajín seasoning (see Trejo's Tip, page 104)

Ground red chile powder to taste

1 cup finely chopped fresh cilantro

Cook the corn in a large pot of boiling water until it's tender, 5 to 7 minutes. Drain the corn and place the ears on a cutting board. Cut the ears in half.

Place the Cotija on a plate. Using a rubber or silicone spatula, spread the Chipotle Crema over all sides of the pieces of corn. Then roll the corn in the Cotija cheese to coat it completely. Sprinkle with Tajín and chile powder to taste. Serve sprinkled with the cilantro.

STREET CORN IN A BOWL

This dish has all the flavors of *elote* but involves more vegetables and a little less Chipotle Crema, making it a bit healthier. The sprinkling of popcorn is a fun way of adding flavor and some crunchy texture without too much fat.

Serves 2 (4 pieces)

- 2 large ears corn, husked
- 2 tablespoons Chipotle Crema (page 60)
- 6 scallions, white and light green parts, thinly sliced
- ½ cup finely chopped fresh cilantro, plus more for serving
- ½ serrano chile, thinly sliced
- 1 garlic clove, minced
- Juice of 1 lime
- 1 cup freshly popped popcorn
- ¼ cup crumbled Cotija cheese

Heat a gas or charcoal grill to medium heat.

Grill the husked corn, turning the ears every few minutes, until the kernels are blistered and the color has gone from pale to bright yellow. Let the corn cool, and then slice the kernels off the cobs.

In a medium bowl, combine the grilled corn, Chipotle Crema, scallions, cilantro, serrano, garlic, and lime juice and mix well. Transfer the salad to a serving bowl and sprinkle with the popcorn, Cotija, and more cilantro.

COTIJA & CHILE MASHED POTATOES

You don't think of mashed potatoes when you think of Mexican food, but the roasted chiles and Cotija cheese make these a good match for the flavors of other dishes in this book. These potatoes are rich, creamy, and indulgent and go well with a steak and Trejo's Steak Sauce (page 54) or alongside *barbacoa* or *carnitas*.

Serves 6

2 medium poblano chiles

2 pounds Yukon Gold potatoes, scrubbed (leave the skin on) and quartered

2 cups whole milk

1 teaspoon kosher salt

1 teaspoon freshly ground black pepper

8 tablespoons (1 stick) unsalted butter, melted

3 tablespoons crumbled Cotija cheese

½ cup shredded Mexican-style cheese blend, store-bought or homemade (see page 86)

Place the chiles directly over a gas burner turned to medium-high and cook, turning them occasionally with tongs, until they are blistered on all sides, about 5 minutes. Let the chiles cool and then scrape off the blackened outer layer with a spoon. Cut off the stems, slice the chiles lengthwise, remove the seeds, and coarsely chop the chiles. You should have about ½ cup. Set aside.

Put the potatoes in a medium saucepan and add cold water to cover. Bring the water to a simmer over high heat, then reduce the heat to medium-low and cook until the potatoes are tender throughout, about 20 minutes. Drain the potatoes and set them aside to cool slightly.

In the same saucepan used for the potatoes, combine the milk, salt, and pepper. Set the pan over medium heat. When the milk is just hot enough that you can see steam rising, return the potatoes to the pan and use a potato masher to combine them with the milk, taking care not to overmix.

Gently stir in the melted butter, and then stir in half of the Cotija, half of the cheese blend, and half of the chopped chiles. Gently mix again.

Use a rubber spatula to transfer the mashed potatoes to a serving dish. Sprinkle with the remaining Cotija, cheese blend, and chiles and serve.

BASIC BLACK BEANS

If you think canned beans are cheap, then wait until you see how far a bag of dried beans can go! With a pound of dried beans that costs a few bucks, you can make enough cooked beans to serve 12 people (or more!), easy. Dried beans tend to have a meatier texture when cooked and will fully soak up the flavors of the ingredients you cook with them. The longer you soak the beans before cooking, the creamier they will get.

Makes 6 cups

- **1 pound dried black beans**
- **2 tablespoons pure olive oil**
- **½ medium yellow or white onion, chopped**
- **2 medium carrots, chopped**
- **1 celery stalk, chopped**
- **½ medium jalapeño, chopped**
- **2 garlic cloves, chopped**
- **1 dried chile de árbol**
- **2 teaspoons ground cumin**
- **1 teaspoon dried oregano**
- **½ cinnamon stick, about 1 inch long**
- **1 dried bay leaf**
- **Kosher salt**
- **1 teaspoon freshly ground black pepper, plus extra to taste**

Place the beans in a large bowl and add enough tepid water to cover them by at least 2 inches. Set aside to soak at room temperature for at least 3 hours and up to overnight.

Heat the oil in a large pot over medium heat until the oil is shimmering but not smoking, about 2 minutes. Add the onion, carrots, celery, jalapeño, and garlic and cook, stirring occasionally, until the vegetables are soft but not browned, 7 to 10 minutes. Drain the beans and add them to the pot along with the chile de árbol, cumin, oregano, cinnamon stick, bay leaf, and salt and pepper. Add cold water to cover the beans by at least 2 inches. Raise the heat to high, bring the water to a boil, then reduce the heat to medium-low and simmer until the beans are tender, adding water if necessary, 45 minutes to 1 hour.

Taste and add more salt and pepper if necessary. Remove and discard the bay leaf, chile de árbol, and cinnamon stick before serving. You can refrigerate the beans in an airtight container for up to 3 days.

SPANISH RICE

Spanish rice, stained yellowish-pink by tomatoes, is a standard side dish in Mexican restaurants across the country. No Combo Platter #3 would be complete without this rice sitting next to some refried beans and whatever else you ordered. We step it up a bit with chile de árbol and organic basmati rice. It's a great burrito filling and a satisfying side to any of the proteins in this book.

Serves 4 to 6

¼ cup plus 2 tablespoons pure olive oil

½ medium white onion, diced

3 garlic cloves, minced

1½ teaspoons kosher salt, plus extra to taste

2 cups basmati rice (preferably organic)

1 cup canned diced tomatoes, with their juices

1 dried chile de árbol

1 dried bay leaf

In a large saucepan, heat ¼ cup of the oil over medium heat until it is shimmering, about 3 minutes. Add the onion and garlic and cook, stirring occasionally, until the onion is translucent, about 5 minutes. Stir in the salt, and then add the basmati rice and toast it, stirring occasionally, until the rice is fragrant, about 5 minutes.

Add 2 cups of water, the tomatoes, the chile de árbol, and the bay leaf and raise the heat to high. Bring the liquid to a boil, then reduce the heat to low. Cover the saucepan and cook the rice for 20 minutes. Turn off the heat and set the pan aside, covered, for 5 minutes.

Uncover the pan, add the remaining 2 tablespoons olive oil, and fluff the rice with a fork. Remove chile and bay leaf. Taste and add more salt if needed.

BROWN BASMATI RICE

When we first opened, this was the rice we served. It has so many spices and so much flavor that by serving it, you're halfway to a healthy meal. As a restaurateur, though, if people don't order it, it isn't worth keeping on the menu, and for whatever reason, everyone requested white or Spanish rice, so we took our healthy brown basmati off the menu. We include it here because it was a staff favorite, and I just know some extremely health-conscious cooks will be extra-happy to have this recipe—this one's for you guys.

Serves 6

2 tablespoons pure olive oil

1 dried chile de árbol

1 tablespoon cumin seeds

½ medium yellow onion, diced

2 garlic cloves, chopped

2 cups brown basmati rice, preferably organic

1 dried bay leaf

2 cups full-fat coconut milk

½ cinnamon stick, about 1 inch

In a medium pot, heat the olive oil over medium-high heat until it is smoking, about 3 minutes. Add the chile and the cumin seeds and toast, stirring often, until they are fragrant, 5 to 10 seconds. Add the onion and cook, stirring often, until it is soft, about 7 minutes. Add the garlic, cook for 1 minute, and then add the rice and bay leaf. Toast the rice, stirring it often, until it smells toasted and becomes opaque, about 5 minutes.

Add 2 cups of water, the coconut milk, and the cinnamon stick and bring the liquid to a boil. Then reduce the heat to low, cover the pot, and simmer for 25 minutes. Remove the pan from the heat and let the rice sit, still covered, for 15 minutes before uncovering and fluffing it with a fork. Discard the chile, bay leaf, and cinnamon stick before serving.

REFRIED BLACK BEANS

This may be the best bang for the buck dish in the entire cookbook. You can used canned beans and make this in about 20 minutes flat and feast for cheap. It's one of those rare dishes that's incredibly hearty and satisfying but still good for you.

Makes about 4 cups

¼ cup pure olive oil

½ medium yellow onion, diced

4 to 5 large garlic cloves, chopped

1 medium jalapeño, chopped

4 cups canned black beans, drained, liquid reserved

2 teaspoons ground cumin

1 teaspoon kosher salt

¼ teaspoon cayenne pepper

Heat a cast-iron skillet over medium-low heat for 2 minutes and then add the olive oil. Add the onion, garlic, and jalapeño and cook until the vegetables are soft but not browned, stirring them occasionally, about 10 minutes.

Add the beans, cumin, salt, and cayenne. Smash the beans with a large fork or a potato masher until you have a mixture of textures: not too chunky, not too smooth. Cook, stirring occasionally, until the mixture is sweetly fragrant and has thickened slightly, about 10 minutes. Taste the beans to check if they're tender. If not, stir in ¼ cup of the reserved bean liquid and cook 5 minutes more and taste again. Add bean liquid until the desired consistency is reached (we make our beans so they are a little thicker than soup; if you run out of bean liquid, add water). Serve immediately or refrigerate in an airtight container for up to 3 days.

MEXICAN-ISH RISOTTO

Unlike the standard rice cooking method, the technique in this recipe calls for gradually adding the liquid, ladleful by ladleful, to make a creamy porridge, sort of like Italian risotto. We add some chile and cinnamon to make it a little Mexican. While this is technically a savory dish, the cinnamon adds just enough of a sweet note that you can add honey, maple syrup, or agave and butter and have it for breakfast. If you're serving it classic-style for dinner, try it with Grilled Spicy Diablo Shrimp (page 118) or pan-fried with chorizo and a fried egg.

Serves 6

1½ cups full-fat coconut milk

2 tablespoons pure olive oil

2 cups short-grain brown rice

½ cup chopped white or yellow onion

2 garlic cloves, chopped

1 tablespoon cumin seeds

1 dried bay leaf

½ cinnamon stick, or ¼ teaspoon ground cinnamon

1 whole dried chile de árbol

Kosher salt

Freshly ground black pepper

In a medium pot set over medium-low heat, combine 3 cups of water with the coconut milk and heat until the liquid is warm. Reduce the heat to low.

In a second medium pot, heat the oil over medium-high heat until it is shimmering, about 2 minutes. Add the rice, onion, garlic, cumin seeds, bay leaf, cinnamon stick, and chile and toast, stirring, until the rice is well coated in the oil and the spices are fragrant, about 2 minutes. Reduce the heat to medium-low.

Add 1 cup of the warm coconut liquid to the rice and stir until it is absorbed, 5 to 8 minutes. Continue to add more liquid, 1 cup at a time, stirring constantly, until the rice is tender (but still a little al dente at the core), 25 to 30 minutes total. Stir in the remaining ½ cup of coconut liquid and season to taste with salt and pepper. Discard the bay leaf, cinnamon stick, and chile before serving.

Number One Fan

In 2019 my Rams made it to the Super Bowl. Did I say mine? I meant ours. The Rams are a true Los Angeles institution. Even though the Rams have been back from St. Louis for only three years, I've been a fan since the 1950s — before they moved away. Before my family moved to Pacoima, we lived in Echo Park. Back then, there was still a streetcar system snaking all over town. My cousins and I would hop on a streetcar and take it downtown to the Los Angeles Memorial Coliseum an hour or so before kickoff. Back then security was pretty lax. We'd hide in the bathrooms and wait for a big rush of ticket holders before sneaking in with them.

Going to watch the Rams and my beloved Dodgers was one of my all-time favorite things to do as a kid, and now when I look back, I see that it was a survival skill and an escape—from school, from juvenile hall, from everything. You were there rooting for your team with what felt like everybody else in the city . . . and the feeling was indescribable. I was just swallowed up in this vortex of energy and nothing mattered more than what was happening in that moment.

I'm still a sports fanatic, maybe even more than I was back then when I watched Dodger Stadium being built. When the Dodgers were playing the Red Sox in the 2018 World Series, one of the games was in the 12th inning and people were beginning to leave and I screamed at them and told them to all sit down. By the 15th inning I was beginning to regret it because now there was no way I could leave. The Dodgers ended up winning in the 18th inning in the longest game in World Series history. I'd like to think I did my part to help them get there.

Now I get to do more than cheer from the stands—I get to use my restaurants to support the teams and feed the fans. When the Dodgers were in the World Series, we put baseball-shaped Dodgers donuts on the menu, and when the Rams were in the Super Bowl, we had football-shaped Rams donuts in the team's colors. I've literally fed the Dodgers and the Rams by taking the Trejo's Taco truck to the teams when they're training. And let me tell you, I've never in my life seen anybody eat more tacos than the Rams!

In 2019, when the Rams played the Patriots at the Super Bowl, we parked a Trejo's Taco truck outside the stadium in Atlanta and gave out free tacos to anyone who wanted to stand in line (and yes, we let the Patriots fans eat, too). I was there wearing my Rams jersey, handing out tacos and taking pictures with fans. When I saw fans from L.A. wearing Trejo's Tacos T-shirts in the crowd—it was like they were using our logo as a way to show their L.A. pride—wow, I was blown away and so proud.

When I was at the Super Bowl, I felt that same amazing energy I had felt sixty years earlier. I couldn't help but think of my dad and the jersey and helmet he bought for me when I was a kid. I was so proud to wear Norm Van Brocklin's number 11 jersey. I wonder what Dad would think of me and the Rams now!

A sign on the truck we took to the Super Bowl in Atlanta read "Feel the Love" and that's kind of what it's all about. Last year, my cousin had just gotten out of prison and we took him to a Dodgers game. He'd done 38 years and he secretly was holding back, trying not to cry. He looked at me and said that he couldn't believe it: "I'm in Dodger fucking stadium, homes." Sports was kind of about getting out of everything, whatever you were going through, whatever was happening. When you were sitting in the Coliseum screaming for the Rams, or just being in Dodger Stadium with all the energy around you, there was nothing else going on. It was a beautiful thing back then, and it's an even more beautiful thing now that I get to use sports to support my friends, my family, and the teams. And believe me, when the Rams are training next year, we'll have our truck out there to feed them.

Donuts

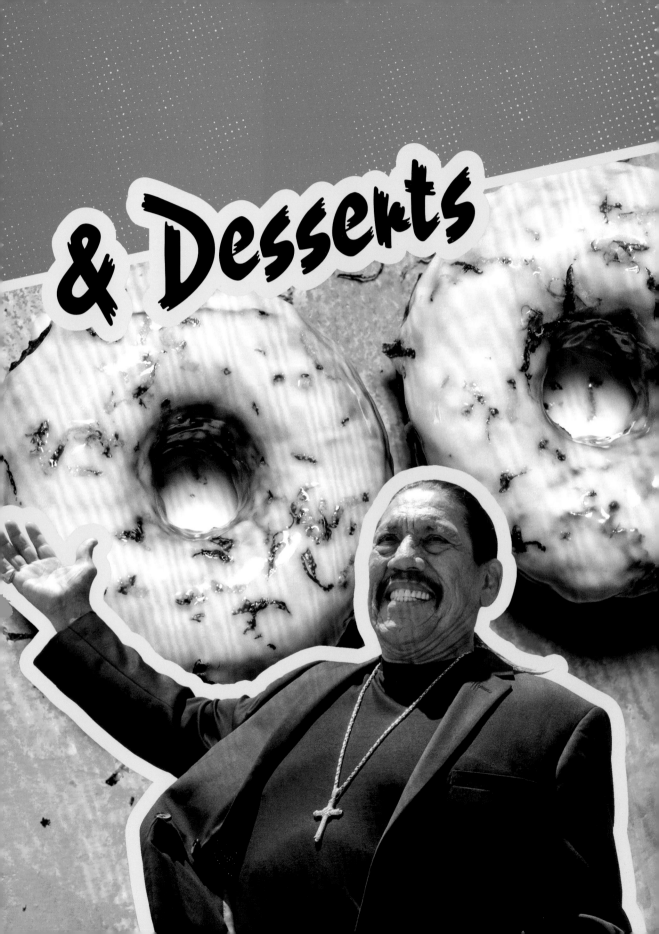

Driving around Los Angeles and looking at the strip malls, you might get the impression that the city's three major food groups are tacos, burgers, and donuts. There are around 700 donut shops in the L.A. area, which is over three times as many as in New York City, and I'm proud to count Trejo's Coffee & Donuts as part of what is arguably the donut capital of the world.

When you're competing with 700 donut shops, you need to stand out. When we opened our store on the corner of Highland Avenue and Santa Monica Boulevard in Hollywood, in a space that used to house an old Donut Time, we could've tried to put a big oversized statue of a donut on our roof, but zoning has gotten a lot tougher than back in the 1950s when oversized food on the roof of restaurants was a thing. So we had the bright idea—literally—to paint the side of our donut shop the color pink. And then graffiti artist Man One painted a 10-foot-high picture of my face on it. Up until that point, pink was not a color typically associated with me, but I'm getting used to it.

You might notice that most of the boxes that donuts come in in Los Angeles are colored pink, too. Like so many L.A. traditions, there's a great immigrant story behind it. It turns out a Cambodian refugee named Ted Ngoy went through the Winchell's Donuts management training program and became a successful donut shop operator on his own, with multiple locations throughout the L.A. area. Over the years he sponsored numerous Cambodian immigrants, who now own 80 percent of the donut shops in L.A. They eventually started using the pink boxes as a more affordable alternative to the then-traditional white boxes. And now pink is the standard color for donut boxes throughout L.A. Who would've thought that a Cambodian immigrant could make a Mexican tough guy like the color pink? It's stories like these that make me love this city. Thank you, Mr. Ngoy.

Donuts are a little like tacos in that you can do anything you want with them in terms of ingredients. If a chef like L.A. homeboy Roy Choi can put Korean bulgogi and kimchi in a tortilla and become famous, and we can turn falafel and chicken tikka masala into tacos and people keep ordering them, then why the hell can't we put ingredients like chiles and cheese and hot sauce inside a donut, or spread a margarita-inspired tequila, lime, and salt glaze on another? Like with the tacos, it's the same for donuts: there are no rules as long as it's delicious.

The team at the donut shop are what I like to think of as artists whose medium isn't paint but sugar. Every day they come up with original daily specials, sometimes riffing off on the season, holidays, or a sporting event like the playoffs (we've done Dodgers, Rams, and Lakers donuts). We've done old-fashioned pumpkin spice–flavored donuts in the fall, heart-shaped donuts for Valentine's Day, passion fruit–glazed ones in the winter, and malted pastry cream–filled donuts with chocolate glaze and buttercream frosting . . . just because. And we've got our vegan friends covered, too, because I see no reason why a vegan shouldn't be able to come by and get a mixed dozen.

The first food I ate out of prison wasn't a taco—it was cookies. My mom and dad barely let me back into the house after I did my first four and a half years. I was convicted of bunco sales, which is the selling of a substance in lieu of narcotics (I was selling sugar even back then!). When I showed up at home, they let me into the house but they wouldn't look at me. They wouldn't talk to me. My dad went back to reading the paper. My mom went into the kitchen. I sat in my room. Nothing had changed. And then I smelled something I hadn't smelled in over four years. You've got to remember—a prison smells like a lot of things, and not many of them are good. What I smelled was sweet and buttery. My mom was *baking*. Sugar cookies. Right then, I knew everything was going to be okay.

Trejo's Tips

STUFF YOU NEED TO MAKE DONUTS

To make donuts, you're going to need some special equipment: You could conceivably make these without the benefit of a stand mixer, but the mixer makes the already labor-intensive process so much easier. You'll also need a deep fryer or a large deep heavy pot to fry in and a candy thermometer or deep-frying thermometer to monitor the temperature. Get a spider strainer to retrieve the donuts out of the oil, and a 3-inch donut cutter. If your cutter doesn't have a built-in hole, you'll need a 1-inch round cutter to create the center hole. You should also get a couple of wire cooling racks.

IT'S TIME TO EAT THE DONUTS

There's a reason donut shops discount their donuts at the end of the day: they're best eaten while they are super fresh. If you're going to dive into a big project like frying up some of these beauties, be sure to time it so that you serve them within 4 hours of making them. If you have any leftover donuts, let them cool completely and store them in an airtight container at room temperature.

TREJO'S DONUTS

Donuts are a no-joke undertaking that take 2 days of work and love. What you get in return is a food that is about as amazing as food can be. Perfection, though, is fleeting, because 4 hours out of the fryer, they lose that magic. Which is why every donut shop in town sells their donuts for half price at the end of the day. Honest to god, they're best enjoyed right out of the fryer. This recipe is for a plain yeasted donut, delicious on its own and the starting point for the Margarita, the Abuelita, and the Lowrider Donuts (pages 187 to 190).

Makes 2 dozen 3-inch donuts and 2 dozen donut holes

½ cup buttermilk

2¼ teaspoons active dry yeast

4 cups sifted all-purpose flour, plus extra for rolling

Scant ½ cup sugar

2 teaspoons kosher salt

8 tablespoons (1 stick) unsalted butter, at room temperature

Scant ¾ cup full-fat sour cream

3 large eggs, beaten

1 teaspoon vanilla extract

2 quarts (8 cups) vegetable oil

MAKE THE DOUGH In a small saucepan set over low heat, warm the buttermilk to 110°F. Remove the pan from the heat and whisk the yeast into the warm buttermilk. Set aside until thickened, about 10 minutes.

Meanwhile, put the flour, sugar, salt, butter, sour cream, eggs, and vanilla in the bowl of a stand mixer.

Add the thickened buttermilk mixture to the mixer bowl, and using the paddle attachment, mix the ingredients together on low speed, stopping every 20 seconds or so to scrape the sides of the bowl, until the mixture is shaggy and no dry ingredients are visible, 1 to 2 minutes. Raise the speed to medium and mix until the dough is well combined and smooth, about 2 minutes. Remove the paddle attachment and switch to the mixer's hook attachment. Knead/mix on medium-low speed for about 5 minutes, until the dough has a smooth and stretchy consistency.

LET THE DOUGH RISE Spray a large bowl with nonstick pan spray (or grease it with a little oil). Transfer the dough to the bowl and lay a sheet of plastic wrap directly on the surface of the dough (this prevents the surface of the dough

recipe continues

from drying out). Set the bowl aside in a draft-free spot and let the dough rise at room temperature until doubled in size, about 2 hours.

Line a sheet pan with parchment paper, and coat it lightly with pan spray. Transfer the dough to the prepared sheet pan. Wrap the dough and sheet pan (together) tightly with plastic wrap and refrigerate overnight.

Remove the dough from the refrigerator and discard the plastic wrap. Transfer the dough to a lightly floured work surface, flour a rolling pin, and roll the dough until it's ½ inch thick. Let it rest for 10 minutes.

Meanwhile, line two sheet pans with parchment paper and flour them generously.

Using a 3-inch donut cutter, stamp out donuts close together (so you don't waste dough). If you don't have a donut cutter, use a 1-inch cookie cutter to stamp out a small round of dough from the center of each donut. Transfer the big donuts and the small donut holes to the prepared sheet pans, placing them a couple of inches apart from each other. Let the donuts proof in a warm, draft-free area until they have increased in size by one-third, about 1 hour.

FRY THE DONUTS   If using a deep fryer, follow the manufacturer's directions to heat the oil to 350°F. (Alternatively, attach a candy thermometer to a large deep heavy-bottomed pot, making sure the tip of the thermometer does not touch the bottom of the pot. Fill the pot with the oil and heat it slowly to 350°F over medium-low heat.) Once the oil reaches this temperature, try to maintain it. If it gets too hot, simply turn the heat down or off until it reduces to 350°F.

Carefully lower no more than 3 donuts at a time into the oil (if you overcrowd the oil with donuts, they'll cool the oil and absorb it—making for greasy, sad donuts). Fry the donuts for about 1 minute on each side, gently turning them over with a spider strainer, until they are golden brown. Remove the cooked donuts with the spider strainer and set them on a wire cooling rack to drain. Let the oil rewarm to 350°F if necessary, then add a few more donuts to the pot. Repeat until all of the donuts are fried.

Follow these same frying instructions for the donut holes, cooking up to 8 at a time and frying both sides until golden brown. Keep in mind that they will need a bit less time to fry than the donuts due to their smaller size. Remove the cooked donut holes with the spider strainer and drain them on a cooling rack. Serve immediately or within 4 hours.

MARGARITA DONUTS

I don't consume alcohol in any form, so that means I don't eat this donut, but people tell me it's amazing. It's our basic yeasted donut with a tequila-lime glaze.

Makes 2 dozen donuts and 2 dozen donut holes

1 recipe fried Trejo's Donuts (page 183), still hot, placed on wire racks

Tequila–Key Lime Glaze

3 cups confectioners' sugar

5 tablespoons fresh Key lime or Persian lime juice

2 tablespoons blanco tequila

1½ teaspoons Lyle's Golden Syrup (see Trejo's Tip), light corn syrup, or honey

Maldon salt, for sprinkling

Grated zest of 2 limes

Sift the confectioners' sugar into a large bowl. In a small bowl, combine the lime juice, tequila, and golden syrup. Add the liquid mixture to the confectioners' sugar and whisk together until smooth.

Using a rubber spatula, spread the glaze over the top half of the donuts. Sprinkle the Maldon salt and lime zest over the glaze. Let the glaze set up, about 5 minutes, and eat the donuts immediately or within 4 hours (see Trejo's Tip, page 182).

Trejo's Tip

LYLE'S GOLDEN SYRUP

A natural sweetener made from the sugarcane refining process, golden syrup is the secret weapon of bakers. It adds a smooth texture and complex sweetness to glazes for our donuts. The best quality is Lyle's Golden Syrup, which originated in England and is now available in supermarkets across the United States and Canada. If you don't have it on hand, you could use light corn syrup or even honey.

THE ABUELITA

A donut topped with two kinds of chocolate—a creamy glaze plus a crunchy crumb topping—is a very good donut. This is another of our top sellers.

Makes 2 dozen donuts and 2 dozen donut holes

1 recipe fried Trejo's Donuts (page 183), still hot, placed on wire racks

Chocolate Crumb Topping

½ cup confectioners' sugar

⅓ cup all-purpose flour

⅓ cup unsweetened Dutch-processed cocoa powder (we use Valrhona)

¼ teaspoon kosher salt

10 tablespoons (1¼ sticks) unsalted butter, cut into ½-inch pieces

Dark Chocolate Glaze

4 cups confectioners' sugar

1½ cups heavy cream

1½ teaspoons Lyle's Golden Syrup (see Trejo's Tip, page 187), light corn syrup, or honey

¼ teaspoon vanilla extract

4½ ounces 70% cacao bittersweet chocolate (we use the Guanaja variety from Valrhona), chopped (about ½ cup)

MAKE THE TOPPING   Preheat the oven to 325°F.

Put the confectioners' sugar, flour, cocoa powder, and salt in the bowl of a food processor and pulse to combine. Add the butter cubes and pulse until the texture looks like a very fine streusel (you don't want to see any chunks of butter—but be careful not to over-blend). Transfer the crumbs to a parchment paper–lined sheet pan and spread them out evenly. Bake until the streusel is lightly toasted, about 15 minutes. Remove the pan from the oven and set it aside to let the topping cool completely. The crumbs will crisp as they cool.

MAKE THE GLAZE   Sift the confectioners' sugar into a large bowl. In a medium bowl, whisk together the cream, golden syrup, and vanilla. Add the liquid mixture to the confectioners' sugar and whisk together until smooth.

Place the chopped chocolate in a microwave-safe bowl and melt it in 30-second bursts, stirring after each, until the chocolate is just melted and smooth. Add the chocolate to the sugar/cream mixture and stir to combine (the glaze will be thick). Set the glaze aside at room temperature.

FINISH THE DONUTS   Using a rubber spatula, spread the glaze on top of the donuts. Sprinkle the chocolate crumble on top and let the glaze set up, about 5 minutes. Serve immediately or within 4 hours of making (see page 182).

THE LOWRIDER
(RAISED DONUTS WITH CINNAMON SUGAR)

This delicious cinnamon-sugar donut is another one of our best sellers.

Makes 2 dozen donuts and 2 dozen donut holes

Cinnamon-Sugar Topping

1 cup sugar

1 teaspoon ground cinnamon

½ teaspoon fine sea salt

1 recipe fried Trejo's Donuts (page 183), still hot, placed on wire racks

In a small bowl, whisk together the sugar, cinnamon, and sea salt. One minute after removing the donuts from the oil, sprinkle them generously with the cinnamon sugar (you want the donuts to be warm so the cinnamon sugar sticks to them). Eat immediately or within 4 hours of making (see Trejo's Tip, page 182).

NACHO DONUTS

If you've never had our Nacho Donut, you're missing out on one of the greatest breakfast inventions of all time. It's a donut. But it's nachos. All in one. It's not too sweet, it's just spicy enough, and it's amazing.

Makes 2 dozen donuts and 2 dozen donut holes

½ cup buttermilk

2¼ teaspoons active dry yeast

4 cups sifted all-purpose flour, plus extra for rolling

⅓ cup sugar

2 teaspoons kosher salt

8 tablespoons (1 stick) unsalted butter, at room temperature

Scant ¾ cup sour cream

3 large eggs, beaten

¾ cup grated cheddar cheese, plus ¾ cup for garnish

1 tablespoon hot sauce, such as Trejo's, Tapatío, or Cholula

½ cup minced roasted poblano chiles (see mashed potatoes on page 168 for method)

2 tablespoons minced fresh chives

2 quarts (8 cups) vegetable oil

MAKE THE DOUGH In a small saucepan set over low heat, warm the buttermilk to 110°F. Remove the pan from the heat and whisk the yeast into the warm buttermilk. Set aside until thickened, about 10 minutes.

Meanwhile, put the flour, sugar, salt, butter, sour cream, eggs, ¾ cup of the cheese, and the hot sauce in the bowl of a stand mixer.

Add the thickened buttermilk mixture to the mixer bowl, and using the paddle attachment, mix the ingredients together on low speed, stopping every 20 seconds or so to scrape the sides of the bowl, until the mixture is shaggy and no dry ingredients are visible, 1 to 2 minutes. Raise the speed to medium and mix until the dough is well combined and smooth, about 2 minutes. Add the minced chiles and chives, and mix until well incorporated, about 1 minute. Remove the paddle attachment and switch to the mixer's hook attachment. Knead/mix on medium-low speed for about 5 minutes, until the dough has a smooth and stretchy consistency.

LET THE DOUGH RISE Spray a large bowl with nonstick pan spray (or grease it with a little oil). Transfer the dough to the bowl and lay a sheet of plastic wrap directly on the surface of the dough (this prevents the surface of the dough from drying out). Set the bowl aside in a draft-free spot and let the dough rise at room temperature until doubled in size, about 2 hours.

recipe continues

Line a sheet pan with parchment paper and coat it lightly with pan spray. Transfer the dough to the prepared sheet pan. Wrap the dough and sheet pan (together) tightly with plastic wrap and refrigerate overnight.

Remove the dough from the refrigerator and discard the plastic wrap. Transfer the dough to a lightly floured work surface, flour a rolling pin, and then roll the dough until it's ½ inch thick. Let it rest for 10 minutes.

Meanwhile, line two sheet pans with parchment paper and flour them generously.

Use a 3-inch donut cutter to stamp out donuts close together (so you don't waste dough). If you don't have a donut cutter, use a 1-inch cookie cutter to stamp out a small round of dough from the center of each donut. Transfer the big donuts and the small donut holes to the prepared sheet pans, placing them a couple of inches apart from each other. Let the donuts proof in a warm, draft-free area until they have increased in size by one-third, about 1 hour.

FRY THE DONUTS If you are using a deep fryer, follow the manufacturer's directions to heat the oil to 350°F. (Alternatively, attach a candy thermometer to a large deep heavy-bottomed pot, making sure the tip of the thermometer does not touch the bottom of the pot. Fill the pot with the oil and heat it slowly to 350°F over medium-low heat.) Once the oil reaches this temperature, try to maintain it. If it gets too hot, simply turn the heat down or off until it reduces to 350°F.

Carefully lower no more than 3 donuts at a time into the oil (if you overcrowd the oil with donuts, they'll cool the oil and absorb it—making for greasy, sad donuts). Fry the donuts for about 1 minute on each side, gently turning them over with a spider strainer, until they are golden brown. Remove the cooked donuts with the spider strainer and set them on a wire cooling rack to drain. While they are still warm, sprinkle the donuts with some of the remaining grated cheese.

Let the oil rewarm to 350°F if necessary, then add a few more donuts to the pot. Repeat until all of the donuts are fried, sprinkling them with cheese while they're still warm.

Follow these same frying instructions for the donut holes, adding up to 8 at a time and frying both sides until golden brown. Keep in mind that they will need a bit less time to fry than the donuts, due to their smaller size. Remove the cooked donut holes with the spider strainer and drain them on a cooling rack. Sprinkle them with the cheese while they're still warm.

Eat the Nacho Donuts and donut holes immediately or within 4 hours of cooking (see Trejo's Tip, page 182).

VEGAN DONUTS

This recipe is for a plain vegan donut, the starting point for the Vegan Coco Loco Donuts and Vegan Berry Donuts (page 197). Our dairy- and egg-free donuts are made with ripe banana, which gives them a tender, cake-like texture. Simply dust these with powdered sugar or top as we do at the shop.

Makes 2 dozen donuts and 2 dozen donut holes

¼ cup solid vegetable shortening

1 cup sugar

1 large ripe banana, peeled and mashed

4 cups cake flour or all-purpose flour, plus extra for rolling

1 teaspoon baking powder

1½ teaspoons salt

Scant ¾ cup almond milk

1 teaspoon apple cider vinegar

1 teaspoon vanilla extract

2 quarts (8 cups) vegetable oil

MAKE THE DOUGH   In the bowl of a stand mixer fitted with the paddle attachment, beat together the shortening and sugar on medium-low speed until the mixture is crumbly, like coarse cornmeal, about 2 minutes. Add the mashed banana and mix on medium-low speed until the ingredients are combined, about 2 minutes.

Combine the flour, baking powder, and salt in a large bowl. In a medium bowl, combine the almond milk, apple cider vinegar, and vanilla. Alternate adding the flour mixture and the almond milk mixture to the banana mixture, mixing until combined and just smooth but not over-mixed, about 3 minutes. Transfer the dough to a floured surface, flour a rolling pin, and roll the dough until it's ¾ inch thick.

Line two sheet pans with parchment paper and flour them generously.

Using a 3-inch donut cutter, stamp out donuts close together (so you don't waste dough). If you don't have a donut cutter, use a 1-inch cookie cutter to stamp out a small round of dough from the center of each donut. Transfer the big donuts and the small donut holes to the prepared sheet pans, about 1 inch apart.

FRY THE DONUTS   If you are using a deep fryer, follow the manufacturer's directions to heat the oil to 350°F. (Alternatively, attach a candy thermometer to a large deep heavy-bottomed pot, making sure the tip of the thermometer does not touch the bottom of the pot. Fill the pot with the oil and heat it slowly to 350°F over medium-low heat.) Once the oil reaches this temperature, try to maintain it. If it gets too hot, simply turn the heat down or off until it reduces to 350°F.

Carefully lower no more than 3 donuts at a time into the oil (if you overcrowd the oil with donuts, they'll cool the oil and absorb it—making for greasy, sad donuts). Fry the donuts for 1 to 2 minutes on each side, gently turning them over with a spider strainer, until they are golden brown. Remove the cooked donuts with the spider strainer and set them on a cooling rack to drain. Let the oil rewarm to 350°F if necessary, then add a few more donuts to the pot. Repeat until all of the donuts are fried.

Follow these same frying instructions for the donut holes, adding up to 8 at a time and frying both sides until golden brown. Keep in mind that they will need a bit less time to fry than the donuts, due to their smaller size. Remove the cooked donut holes with the spider strainer and drain them on a cooling rack. Serve immediately or within 4 hours (see Trejo's Tip, page 182).

VEGAN BERRY DONUTS

They say you eat with your eyes, and this pink beauty is as delicious as it looks. If you can't find blueberry juice, feel free to substitute grape juice.

Makes 2 dozen donuts and 2 dozen donut holes

Vegan Berry Glaze

4 cups confectioners' sugar

2 teaspoons Lyle's Golden Syrup (see Trejo's Tip, page 187), light corn syrup, or honey

½ cup berry jam (mixed berry or raspberry)

¼ cup blueberry juice

¼ cup unsweetened almond milk

1 recipe fried Vegan Donuts (page 194), still hot, placed on wire racks

MAKE THE GLAZE Combine the confectioners' sugar, golden syrup, berry jam, blueberry juice, and almond milk in a large bowl, whisking until completely smooth.

GLAZE THE DONUTS Using a rubber spatula, spread the glaze over the top half of the donuts and allow the glaze to set up, about 5 minutes. Serve immediately or within 4 hours (see Trejo's Tip, page 182).

VEGAN COCO LOCO DONUTS

This vegan donut gets a double hit of coconut flavor from the sweet Coco Lopez glaze and a toasted coconut topping.

Makes 2 dozen donuts and 2 dozen donut holes

Coco Loco Glaze

2½ cups confectioners' sugar

Scant ½ cup Coco Lopez coconut cream (mix well before measuring)

1½ teaspoons Lyle's Golden Syrup (see Trejo's Tip, page 187), light corn syrup, or honey

Toasted Coconut Topping

1½ cups shredded unsweetened coconut

1 recipe fried Vegan Donuts (page 194), still hot, placed on wire racks

MAKE THE GLAZE Combine the confectioners' sugar, coconut cream, golden syrup, and 1½ tablespoons water in a large bowl and whisk until completely smooth.

MAKE THE TOPPING Place the coconut in a large skillet and cook it over medium-low heat, stirring frequently, until the flakes are mostly golden brown, about 3 minutes. Transfer the coconut to a large plate and let it cool completely.

GLAZE THE DONUTS Using a rubber spatula, spread the glaze over the top half of the donuts. Sprinkle the donuts with the toasted coconut topping and allow the glaze to set up, about 5 minutes. Serve immediately or within 4 hours (see Trejo's Tip, page 182).

MEXICAN HOT CHOCOLATE COOKIES

Here you have all the comforting, warming, and spicy flavors of Mexican hot chocolate in chocolate chocolate-chip cookie form. It's essentially a double chocolate chip cookie that we dust with cinnamon sugar spiked with cayenne. This makes it taste like a chocolate version of the old-fashioned Red Hots candy.

Makes 24 cookies

Cookie Dough

2¼ cups all-purpose flour

½ cup unsweetened Dutch-processed cocoa powder (such as Valrhona)

2 teaspoons cream of tartar

1 teaspoon baking soda

½ teaspoon kosher salt

1 cup (2 sticks) unsalted butter, at room temperature

1½ cups sugar

2 large eggs

½ cup semisweet chocolate chips

Cinnamon-Chile Sugar

½ cup sugar

2 tablespoons ground cinnamon

½ teaspoon cayenne pepper

MAKE THE DOUGH Preheat the oven to 400°F.

Set a fine-mesh sieve over a medium bowl. Add the flour, cocoa powder, cream of tartar, baking soda, and salt to the sieve, and sift into the bowl.

In the bowl of a stand mixer fitted with the paddle attachment, beat the butter and sugar together on medium-low speed to combine. Increase the speed to high and beat, scraping down the sides and bottom of the bowl as needed, until light and creamy, about 1 minute. Reduce the speed to medium-low and add the eggs, one at a time, beating well on medium-high after each addition. Reduce the speed to medium-low and add the flour mixture, a little at a time, until there aren't any pockets of flour remaining. Reduce the speed to low, slowly add the chocolate chips, and mix until they are evenly dispersed, about 30 seconds. Scrape down the sides and bottom of the bowl.

MAKE THE CINNAMON-CHILE SUGAR In a shallow soup bowl or on a dinner plate, stir together the sugar, cinnamon, and cayenne until thoroughly mixed. Set aside.

BAKE THE COOKIES Line a sheet pan with parchment paper. Form 2 tablespoons of the cookie dough into a ball (about the size of a Ping-Pong ball) and roll it in the cinnamon-chile sugar topping. Repeat with the remaining dough. Place the balls on the parchment paper–lined sheet pan, spacing them 3 inches apart (you will need to bake the cookies in batches). Bake the cookies until they've flattened and are just set, about 12 minutes, rotating the pan halfway through baking.

Remove the pan from the oven, transfer the cookies to a wire rack, and let them cool completely before serving. Store the cooled cookies in an airtight container for up to 3 days.

RICE PUDDING

This is a rich, creamy, and decadent dish that we serve cold at the restaurant. It makes a great dessert or even a sugary boost to the day at breakfast.

Makes 5 cups

- 1½ cups arborio rice
- 2 quarts (8 cups) whole milk
- ½ cup sugar
- ¼ teaspoon ground cinnamon, plus extra for serving
- ¼ teaspoon kosher salt
- 2 large eggs
- ½ cup heavy cream
- 1 teaspoon vanilla extract
- ½ teaspoon freshly grated nutmeg

In a large pot, combine the rice, milk, sugar, cinnamon, and salt. Cook over medium heat, stirring often, until the mixture begins to bubble rapidly. Then reduce the heat to medium-low and simmer gently, stirring often, until the mixture is slightly thicker than cream, 30 to 45 minutes.

Meanwhile, in a small bowl, whisk together the eggs and the cream.

Once the rice is cooked, whisk in the cream mixture and stir for about 3 minutes, until slightly thickened. Remove the pot from the heat. Stir in the vanilla and nutmeg. Let the rice pudding cool to room temperature and serve it with extra cinnamon on top, or transfer it to an airtight container and refrigerate it to serve chilled. The rice pudding will keep for up to 3 days in the refrigerator.

CHURROS

If you don't love churros, the ridged, crispy, but tender donut-like Mexican treat, you're not human. Sorry. (And if you're allergic to gluten, that's no excuse, either: you can make these with gluten-free flour instead of wheat flour!) Churros are all things good about dessert: cinnamony, crunchy, cakey, salty, sweet, fried, handheld.

Yes, these are a bit of a project. But churros are worth it because, at the end of the day, you're going to have homemade hot churros in your own home! One tip to help you streamline: you can make the batter and pipe out little uncooked churros onto a baking sheet lined with parchment paper and freeze them a week or so before you're going to cook them. That way all you have to do when you want to serve them is fry them up and toss them in cinnamon sugar. Just like that, you're a hero.

Makes about twenty 5-inch churros

1 cup (2 sticks) unsalted butter

1 cup sugar

2 teaspoons kosher salt

2 cups all-purpose flour

2 teaspoons vanilla extract

6 large eggs

1 quart (4 cups) canola oil

2 tablespoons ground cinnamon

MAKE THE CHURRO BATTER Place the butter, ½ cup of the sugar, the salt, and 2 cups of water in a medium pot and bring to a boil over medium heat, stirring, until the butter and sugar are melted. Remove the pan from the heat and let the mixture cool until its temperature falls below 125°F on an instant-read thermometer (you don't want the eggs to scramble when you add them to the liquid).

Off the heat, add the flour all at once and mix vigorously with a wooden spoon to incorporate it until the mixture forms a loose batter.

Transfer the churro batter to the bowl of a stand mixer. Using the paddle attachment, beat the batter on medium-low speed for a few seconds just to let off some heat. Add the vanilla, then add the eggs, 2 at a time, scraping the sides of the bowl with a rubber spatula after each addition. Beat until the eggs are fully incorporated and the dough is smooth and a little stretchy. Transfer the dough to a large pastry bag fitted with a #828 star tip.

FRY THE CHURROS Set a wire rack on a sheet pan or line a sheet pan with a double layer of paper towels.

In a large deep pot or a deep fryer, heat the canola oil to 365°F. Once the oil is hot, hold the pastry bag a few inches above the oil and pipe a 5-inch length of dough directly into the hot oil, moving the bag across the oil as you pipe (use your finger or the tip of a knife to break off the dough from the piping bag). Repeat one or two times (you don't want to overcrowd the pot). Fry the churros until they are golden brown, about 1 minute on each side. Use a frying spider to transfer the churros to the prepared sheet pan. Repeat, piping more dough into the hot oil, until you have used all the dough.

Add the remaining ½ cup sugar and the cinnamon to a small paper bag and shake to combine. Add a still-warm churro to the bag and shake lightly to evenly coat the churro on all sides (you want it warm so the cinnamon sugar will stick). Place it on a serving platter. Repeat with the remaining churros and topping.

Churros are awesome eaten warm, or preferably within 1 hour of frying.

Margaritas & Other Drinks

At most Mexican restaurants in L.A., you're going to see big plastic tubs of electric-colored *aguas frescas*: watermelon, lime, orange, and Jamaica (hibiscus). To a kid it's a rainbow of potential sugar highs. A lot of restaurants use a powdered mix, so the drink is not that far off from Kool-Aid, but at our restaurants we make them with fresh juices and cane sugar.

We take the same approach with our *horchata*. Every Mexican has a favorite horchata and a specific idea of how it should taste, like how much cinnamon and how thick and how sweet. Now, I'm not saying that horchata is exactly a health drink, like green tea or kombucha, but we make it a little healthier by using dates (grown in the desert near Palm Springs) as a natural sweetener instead of relying only on corn syrup or white sugar. It adds an unbelievable richness to it. When the restaurant was dialing in the recipe, I tasted it and thought it was pretty good: sweet, rich, cinnamony. But my daughter thought it was a little too light. So the kitchen crew upped the amount of rice, one of the traditional ingredients, and we tasted it, and she was right. Now it's one of the best horchatas in town.

I haven't drunk alcohol for over fifty years, but I drink lots of coffee. And we've got our own custom-roasted blend of coffee at Trejo's Cantina and in the donut shops. L.A. loves its fancy coffees, but my taste for coffee was developed when I was in prison: we'd make it by folding a paper towel into a cone shape and placing it in a cup, filling it with coffee grounds smuggled from the commissary, and pouring hot water through it. That was it. When we had instant coffee, we would mix it with water in a cup and heat it up with a thing we called a stinger, which was basically a heating element you plugged into the wall. You'd stick it in your coffee cup and it would boil the water. It was hot enough to burn your tongue. That's why I like my coffee so hot. It should go without saying that the coffee we serve at Trejo's Donuts is much, *much* better than what we had in prison, but when I do a quality-control check, the temperature of the coffee is the first thing I notice. Old habits die hard.

The Cantinas are meant to be gathering places as much as eating spots, so they all have full bars and different vibes depending on their locations. When you come to the Cantina in Hollywood, it's a place you want to hang out in, with a bar and TVs with the games (yes, plural!) on. Our Cantina in Pasadena is in the same building as the historic Playhouse and it's more upscale. It's always slammed during pre-theater hours with people who will be going to the Playhouse to see a performance. I've seen strangers grab a drink and a bite at the bar before a show and become friends by the end of their meal. In that spirit, the drinks in this chapter are designed to be festive and to be shared, whether it's a margarita or horchata.

CUCUMBER CILANTRO MARGARITA

This is a refreshing, summery spin on a margarita. "Muddling" is a fancy term for smashing vegetables and herbs to release their juices and essential oils. In this case you smash a few pieces of cucumber and a sprig of cilantro in a cocktail shaker before adding the alcohol. You can buy a drinks muddler designed specifically for the task, or you can just use the end of a wooden spoon to do the mashing. Shaking the cocktail vigorously for 4 seconds is crucial, not just to cool down the drink and incorporate the ingredients, but also to melt a little of the ice so it dilutes the drink slightly and brings all the flavors into balance.

Makes 1 margarita

Kosher salt, optional

4 thin slices cucumber, plus a ¼-inch-thick slice for garnish

2 sprigs fresh cilantro

½ cup ice cubes

2 ounces (¼ cup) silver tequila

1 ounce (2 tablespoons) fresh lime juice

½ ounce (1 tablespoon) agave syrup

½ ounce (1 tablespoon) Bols Triple Sec

To salt the rim of your glass, fill a shallow bowl with water. On a small plate, pour a circle of salt. Dip the rim of a rocks glass or margarita glass in the water, then dip it into the salt and set it aside.

In the bottom of a cocktail shaker, muddle the 4 cucumber slices with 1 cilantro sprig until the cucumber releases most of its juices and the cilantro is smashed and fragrant. Add the ice cubes, tequila, lime juice, agave syrup, and triple sec. Cover and shake vigorously for 4 seconds. Pour the drink, including the ice, into the glass. Serve the margarita garnished with the remaining cucumber slice and cilantro sprig.

Trejo's Tip

PRE-BATCHING COCKTAILS FOR A PARTY

Making one or two drinks from scratch is one thing, but when you're throwing a party you don't want to be playing bartender all night long. Pre-batching is a caterer trick that cuts down on the drink-making when the party is in full swing. While you can't pre-batch the Cucumber-Cilantro Margarita or Red Chile Margarita, many of the other drinks in this chapter are easy to scale up and make in advance. Simply multiply the liquid ingredients by the number of drinks you want to serve, and mix them in a large bowl or pitcher. Load up an ice bucket. Set up your garnishes. And come party time, simply load a glass with ice, ladle or pour in the liquid ingredients, garnish, and serve.

PINEAPPLE CINNAMON MARGARITA

HIBISCUS MARGARITA

RED CHILE MARGARITA

RED CHILE MARGARITA

We muddle red Fresno chiles into this spicy margarita to give it a kick, and then we garnish it with Tajín seasoning—the slightly spicy, tangy, and salty powder you see street-corner fruit vendors in L.A. sprinkling on cut fruit. If you can't find Fresnos, you can use jalapeños, which are slightly hotter.

Makes 1 margarita

Kosher salt, optional

2 to 3 thin slices Fresno chile, plus 1 extra slice for garnish

½ cup ice cubes

2 ounces (¼ cup) silver tequila

1 ounce (2 tablespoons) fresh lime juice, plus 1 lime wheel for garnish

½ ounce (1 tablespoon) agave syrup

¾ ounce (1½ tablespoons) Bols Triple Sec

Tajín seasoning, to taste (see page 104)

To salt the rim of your drink, fill a shallow bowl with water. On a small plate, pour a circle of salt. Dip the rim of a rocks glass or margarita glass in the water, then dip it into the salt and set it aside.

In the bottom of a cocktail shaker, muddle the Fresno chile slices until slightly smashed and they release their juices. Add the ice, tequila, lime juice, agave syrup, and triple sec. Cover and shake vigorously for 4 seconds. Pour all of the ingredients, including the ice, into the glass. Sprinkle the top of the drink with Tajín, and garnish it with the lime wheel and chile slice.

Trejo's Tip

For even more great flavor, add 2 tablespoons of Tajín seasoning to the salt before dipping the rim of the glass in it.

LAVENDER MARGARITA

This is a very Los Angeles spin on the margarita. Some people might associate lavender with exotic locales in the South of France, but the fragrant flower almost grows wild in front yards and on parkways in Los Angeles. We double the lavender flavoring here by using both lavender syrup and lavender bitters. You can easily buy Torani lavender syrup online, as well as any number of brands of lavender bitters. If you want to make this drink even more Angeleno, use the Greenbar Distillery's Bar Keep lavender bitters, which are organic and are made in downtown L.A.

Makes 1 margarita

½ cup ice cubes

2 ounces (¼ cup) silver tequila

1 ounce (2 tablespoons) fresh lime juice

½ ounce (1 tablespoon) lavender syrup

½ ounce (1 tablespoon) Bols Triple Sec

3 to 4 dashes lavender bitters

Edible lavender buds, optional

In a cocktail shaker, combine the ice, tequila, lime juice, lavender syrup, triple sec, and bitters. Cover and shake vigorously for 4 seconds. Pour the ingredients, including the ice, into a rocks glass. Garnish with the lavender buds, if using.

PINEAPPLE CINNAMON MARGARITA

Sweet and tangy pineapple and warming cinnamon make this margarita a vacation in a glass. Leave out the tequila and triple sec for a refreshing—yet unpredictable—non-alcoholic drink.

Makes 1 margarita

- ½ cup ice cubes
- 2 ounces (¼ cup) silver tequila
- ½ ounce (1 tablespoon) pineapple juice
- ½ ounce (1 tablespoon) fresh lime juice
- ½ ounce (1 tablespoon) agave syrup
- ½ ounce (1 tablespoon) Bols Triple Sec
- ¼ teaspoon ground cinnamon, plus more for garnish
- 1 pineapple wedge, for garnish

In a cocktail shaker, combine the ice, tequila, pineapple juice, lime juice, agave syrup, triple sec, and cinnamon. Cover and shake vigorously for 4 seconds. Pour the drink, including the ice, into a rocks glass. Garnish with a few dashes of ground cinnamon and the pineapple wedge.

LIME IN THE COCONUT MARGARITA

If you like piña coladas, you'll love this rich and sweet double-coconut margarita. Instead of a salted rim, this drink gets garnished with a rim of shredded coconut.

Makes 1 margarita

- Shredded sweetened coconut
- ½ cup ice cubes
- 2 ounces (¼ cup) silver tequila
- ¾ ounce (1½ tablespoons) fresh lime juice, plus 1 lime wheel for garnish
- 1 ounce (2 tablespoons) Coco Lopez coconut cream
- ½ ounce (1 tablespoon) Bols Triple Sec

Fill a shallow bowl with water. On a small plate, pour a circle of shredded coconut. Dip the rim of a rocks glass or margarita glass in the water, then dip it into the coconut and set it aside.

In a cocktail shaker, combine the ice, tequila, lime juice, coconut cream, and triple sec. Cover and shake vigorously for 4 seconds. Pour the drink, including the ice, into the prepared glass. Garnish with the lime wheel.

HIBISCUS MARGARITA

In addition to making a delicious *agua fresca*, hibiscus, also called *flor de Jamaica*, makes a mean margarita. While we make our own hibiscus syrup and garnish the drink with a hibiscus flower to make it extra-fancy, you can also make the syrup with Red Zinger or other bagged tea made with hibiscus. Don't worry—your marg will still taste amazing.

Makes 1 margarita

½ cup ice cubes

2 ounces (¼ cup) silver tequila

½ ounce (1 tablespoon) hibiscus syrup (see sidebar)

½ ounce (1 tablespoon) fresh lime juice

½ ounce (1 tablespoon) agave syrup

½ ounce (1 tablespoon) Bols Triple Sec

Hibiscus flower or lime wheels, for garnish (optional)

In a cocktail shaker, combine the ice, tequila, hibiscus syrup, lime juice, agave syrup, and triple sec. Cover and shake vigorously for 4 seconds. Pour the drink, including the ice, into a rocks glass. Garnish with a hibiscus flower or lime wheels, if using.

MICHELADA

Sometimes people want a drink, but don't want to drink too much, if you know what I'm saying. A michelada is a great compromise. It's sort of like a low-alcohol Mexican bloody mary.

Makes 4 micheladas

1½ cups tomato juice

⅓ cup lime juice, from 3 to 4 limes, plus 1 lime wedge, for the rims of the glasses, and 4 lime wheels, for garnish

2 teaspoons Worcestershire sauce

1½ teaspoons hot sauce

2 tablespoons kosher salt

2 tablespoons Tajín seasoning (see page 104)

2 bottles of light Mexican beer

Freshly ground black pepper

In a pitcher, combine the tomato juice, lime juice, Worcestershire sauce, and hot sauce.

Mix the salt and Tajín seasoning on a small plate. Run the lime wedge around the rim of each glass, then dip each rim in the mixture.

Fill the glasses halfway with ice. Divide the tomato juice mixture evenly between the glasses. Top with beer and gently stir. Add a pinch of pepper to each drink, garnish each glass with a lime wheel, and serve.

TREJO'S DIY HIBISCUS SYRUP

There are two ways you can make this: with dried hibiscus flowers, which you can get at Mexican markets or online through Amazon, or with Red Zinger or another hibiscus-based herbal tea. In a medium saucepan, combine 1 cup water and 1 cup sugar and bring to a boil. Remove the pan from the heat. Add 1 cup dried hibiscus flowers or 4 hibiscus tea bags to the hot water and let steep for 10 minutes. Strain the flowers or remove the tea bags, and let the syrup cool. It will keep for up to 1 week in the refrigerator.

STRAWBERRY LEMONADE

This is ridiculously easy to make and ten times more delicious than any soda or soft drink that comes in a can. You're going to want to break out your electric juicer for this one.

Makes six 8-ounce servings

1 pound fresh
  strawberries, hulled
  (about 3 cups)

2 cups fresh lemon juice
  (from 8 to 10 lemons)

1 cup sugar

6 slices of lime, for
  garnish (optional)

In a blender, combine the strawberries, lemon juice, and sugar and puree until smooth. Strain the puree through a fine-mesh strainer into a large pitcher. Add 4 cups of water and stir to combine. Chill, and serve in tall glasses over ice, each glass garnished with a slice of lime, if using.

DATE-SWEETENED HORCHATA

The rich and sweet cinnamon-flavored rice drink *horchata* is like dessert in a glass. A lot of the horchata you buy in stores and restaurants is sweetened with corn syrup. Ours gets most of its sweetness from sugary dates grown in the desert. When you store this in the refrigerator, it will separate, so just stir it before serving. You need to start this a day in advance of serving.

Makes about ten 8-ounce servings

1½ pounds (about 4 cups) pitted dried Medjool dates

1 pound basmati rice, rinsed and drained

½ cup sugar

1 cinnamon stick, plus extra for garnish (optional)

Zest of 1 lemon, removed with a vegetable peeler

6 cups unsweetened Califia Barista Blend almond milk

Put the dates in a large bowl and add water to cover. Cover the bowl with plastic wrap and set the dates aside at room temperature to soak overnight.

The next day, combine the rice with 4 cups of hot water in a large bowl. Let sit for at least 2 hours at room temperature.

Drain the soaked dates and put them in a stockpot. Add 3 cups of room-temperature water, the sugar, the cinnamon stick, and the lemon peel. Bring the water to a boil, stir until the sugar dissolves, and then remove the pot from the heat.

Transfer the rice and its soaking water to a blender and blend until smooth. Strain the puree through a fine-mesh sieve into a large bowl to make rice milk.

Remove the cinnamon stick and lemon peel from the date mixture. Put the date mixture in the blender and puree until smooth. Strain the date puree through the sieve into the bowl containing the strained rice water. Let the mixture cool to room temperature, and then add the almond milk. Stir to combine and refrigerate until cold.

Serve the horchata over ice, garnished with cinnamon sticks, if using. It will keep in the refrigerator for up to 3 days.

ACKNOWLEDGMENTS

First and foremost, I'd like to thank my Trejo's Tacos partners, Ash Shah and Jeff Georgino, as well as the entire Trejo's Tacos staff and family, past and present. That includes Josh Rosenstein, Daniel Mattern, Mason Royal, Mark Hendrix, Roxana Jullapat, and Jesyka Washburn.

A shout-out to the bookmakers: Hugh Garvey, Ed Anderson, and Lilian Kang; the entire team at Clarkson Potter, including Raquel Pelzel, Lily Ertischek, Jen Wang, Stephanie Huntwork, Mark McCauslin, Nick Patton, and Kelli Tokos; and Ernesto Yerena and Ken Garduno for their illustrations.

I'm equally grateful for the support of my crew Mariette Matekel, Mario Castillo, Michael Castillo, Bela Lehoczky, Ermahn Ospina, Jay West, and Thomas Brackey. I couldn't do it without any of you.

A special thank-you to my fans who come to the restaurants once for the novelty, but then continue to honor me with their return visits and friendship.

To Eddie Bunker and George Perry, who continue to watch my back from Heaven. I miss our dinners at The Pantry.

Finally, to the glue that keeps it all together, my longtime agent and friend, Gloria Hinojosa, and the entire team at Amsel, Eisenstadt, Frazier & Hinojosa, Inc. Thank you, G-$!

INDEX

ISBN 978-1-9848-2685-5
Ebook ISBN 978-1-9848-2686-2

Printed in China

Book and cover design by Jen Wang
Photographs by Ed Anderson

Illustrations by Ernesto Yerena (page 224)
and Ken Garduno (page 36)

10 9 8 7 6 5 4

First Edition